The Covenant Household

The Covenant Household

DOUGLAS WILSON

CANON  PRESS

MOSCOW, IDAHO

Library of Congress Cataloging-in-Publication Data forthcoming.

22 23 24 25 26 27 28 29 30 21   10 9 8 7 6 5 4 3 2 1

Contents

CHAPTER 1

The Meaning of Federal Marriage

We live in a time when there is much confusion in the unbelieving world about what marriage even is. We do not know what boys and girls are anymore, and thus we do not know what marriage and the family are supposed to be anymore either. We think that we can have our courts just make a decision and so they determine what the family is. As Christians, however, we believe that marriage is something that God created, which means that God establishes and defines it in Genesis.

And Genesis 1:27 says, "So God created man in his own image, in the image of God created he him;

male and female created he them" (emphasis added). Back then, when there were only two people, it was pretty easy to keep track of everybody, and to know exactly what was going on. However, now that there are billions of us, it is easy to get distracted and confused about what humanity is even supposed to be. And this is why covenantal thinking is needed in order for us to make sense of it. To unpack this, let me give you a couple of illustrations.

Do you think of the human race as a big box full of individual ball bearings? If you were to reach into that box and pick up any little ball bearing, you could pull one out without pulling out any of the others. This is because none of them has a relationship to the others beyond physical proximity—they were all in the same box, and that is all. Do you think of yourself as a discrete, stand-alone individual like *that*, or do you think of yourself as an individual leaf on a tree? You can certainly distinguish one leaf from another, but the two leaves are still connected to one another and are part of the same tree.

We are not so much individuals as *inter*-dividuals. We are interconnected. As we work through what the Bible teaches about the covenant, keep this in mind— and a lot of other things will come into focus.

We are interconnected by means of covenants, and so we should note what a covenant actually is. A covenant is a solemn bond, sovereignly administered, with attendant blessings and curses. Understanding this will aid us greatly as we seek to understand the nature of the biblical family.

THE FACE OF MARRIAGE COVENANTS

For various reasons, the word *federal* is grossly misunderstood today. We call our centralized, highly bureaucratic government the *federal* government, and so we think that the word *federal* means bureaucratic, centralized, overgrown, and inefficient. If you use the word *federal*, a lot of people just think of tyrannical swollenness. But more positively, we also tend to think of things that have stability and security. When a bank adds the word *federal* to its name, it is trying to communicate that your money is safe with them.

However, this is not what the word *federal* originally meant. It comes from the Latin word *foedus*, meaning covenant. So, when we talk about federal unions or confederated associations, we are describing groups bound by covenant oaths and covenant loyalties. As Reformed Christians, we should know how important covenants are in the Bible, and this is why we also need to think about covenant families and covenantal marriages.

For example, we can see covenant thinking in Paul: "But I would have you know, that the head of every man is Christ; and the head of the woman is the man; and the head of Christ is God" (1 Cor. 11:3). Central to covenant is the idea of headship. We also see this in Ephesians:

> Wives, submit yourselves unto your own husbands, as unto the Lord. For the husband is the head of the wife, even as Christ is the head of the church: and he is the savior of the body. Therefore as the church is subject unto Christ, so let the wives be to their own husbands in every thing. Husbands, love your wives, even as Christ also loved the church, and gave himself for it; that he might sanctify and cleanse it with the washing of water by the word, that he might present it to himself a glorious church, not having spot, or wrinkle, or any such thing; but that it should be holy and without blemish. So ought men to love their wives as their own bodies. He that loveth his wife loveth himself. For no man ever yet hated his own flesh; but nourisheth and cherisheth it, even as the Lord the church: For we are members of his body, of his flesh, and of his bones. For this cause shall a man leave his father and mother, and shall be joined unto his wife, and they two shall be one flesh. This is a great mystery: but I speak concerning Christ and the church. Nevertheless let every

one of you in particular so love his wife even as himself; and the wife see that she reverence her husband. (Eph. 5:22–33)

Now some Christians might want to charge us with simply having covenant theology on the brain—we have our covenant hammer, and everything looks like a covenant nail. However, the word *testament* is simply another word for covenant. The theme of covenant is so pervasive in Scripture that our Bibles are divided into the old and new covenants.

So how does this bear on the subject of marriage? In Proverbs 2, we have a description of the immoral woman: "When wisdom entereth into thine heart, and knowledge is pleasant unto thy soul; discretion shall preserve thee, understanding shall keep thee: to deliver thee from the way of the evil man, from the man that speaketh froward things; who leave the paths of uprightness, to walk in the ways of darkness; who rejoice to do evil, and delight in the frowardness of the wicked; whose ways are crooked, and they froward in their paths: to deliver thee from the strange woman, even from the stranger which flattereth with her words; which forsaketh the guide of her youth, *and forgetteth the covenant of her God*" (vv. 11–17, emphasis added). In this place adultery is described as forgetting the covenant of your God. The adulterous woman has forsaken the companion of her youth and forgotten the *covenant* that bound her together with him.

If we look at Malachi, we find the men of Israel complaining to the Lord about why their prayers are not answered:

> And this have ye done again, covering the altar of the Lord with tears, with weeping, and with crying out, insomuch that he regardeth not the offering any more, or receiveth it with good will at your hand. Yet ye say, Wherefore? Because the Lord hath been witness between thee and the wife of thy youth, against whom thou hast dealt treacherously: *yet is she thy companion, and the wife of thy covenant.* And did not he make one? Yet had he the residue of the spirit. And wherefore one? That he might seek a godly seed. Therefore take heed to your spirit, and let none deal treacherously against the wife of his youth. For the Lord, the God of Israel, saith that he hateth putting away: for one covereth violence with his garment, saith the Lord of hosts: therefore take heed to your spirit, that ye deal not treacherously. (Mal. 2:13–16, emphasis added)

The men of Israel in Malachi were doing the same thing as the adulterous woman in Proverbs: dealing treacherously with the companion of their youth. We also see here that God hates divorce because in marriage God brings together man and woman to make them one by means of a covenant; it is a covenant that makes her your wife, and so if there is no covenant, there is no marriage.

THE MEANING OF FEDERAL HEADSHIP

The Bible gives us two important examples of federal headship. The first one we see is Adam. None of us has ever met Adam or seen him, but he nevertheless represented us. When Adam was standing there in the Garden, deciding whether or not to eat the forbidden fruit, the entire human race was standing there in the Garden, too.

The other federal head is Jesus Christ. When we speak of the substitutionary death of Jesus, we are explaining how Jesus's death two thousand years ago outside Jerusalem applies to us. On its own, this makes no sense: why would God let us off just because of Christ's death? If God just decided to randomly punish Jesus for our sins, it would be unjust. However, if Jesus died as your covenant representative, then when He died, you died. When He was buried, you were buried. When He rose again, you rose. If He does this as your representative, then there is no injustice involved. Killing an innocent man instead of the guilty makes no moral sense unless that innocent man is a covenant representative. But if there is an organic covenant connection, the picture changes.

To believe this, though, you need a different paradigm for what the human race actually is. If every individual in the world is unrelated to anyone else, then it makes no sense to take some sin that one person commits and punish someone else for it.

Here is another analogy. Since we cannot all go to Washington to vote in Congress, because there would be too many of us, we elect a representative, and he goes to Washington as our substitute. When he votes, I vote. When he acts, I act. When he participates, I participate. Jesus is that kind of representative.

Paul says in Galatians 2:20, "I am crucified with Christ: nevertheless I live; yet not I, but Christ liveth in me: and the life which I now live in the flesh I live by the faith of the Son of God, who loved me, and gave himself for me." When Jesus died, I died. When Jesus was buried, I was buried. When Jesus rose, I rose. We participate in Christ, and Christ is our representative head.

The same thing is true of our relationship to Adam. The Bible says that we are organically connected to him by covenant. Hosea 6:7 says, "But they like men have transgressed the covenant: there have they dealt treacherously against me." The Hebrew word for man here is *adam*, which means you could also translate this as "but they like Adam have transgressed the covenant." When Adam rebelled, all mankind rebelled, and since you are *part* of mankind, you are represented in Adam and his sin. Before you could read, you were probably clonking some other poor kid over the head in the nursery with a hard toy. All of us were sinning before we transitioned to solid food. You are thrust into this world and find yourself sinning before you can even explain what sin is. This is because of Adam's sin. Not only did Adam represent us, but he represented us *well*, so there is no injustice in being born into a sinful race.

It is striking that the Bible describes Christ as a second Adam in both 1 Corinthians and Romans. We got into this mess through an Adam, and we can only get out of it through another Adam: in the final analysis you must be represented either by the first Adam or by the second. Just as the sin of the first Adam condemned us, so also the obedience of the second Adam rescued us: "Nevertheless death reigned from Adam to Moses, even over them that had not sinned after the similitude of Adam's transgression, who is the figure of him that was to come. But not as the offence, so also is the free gift. For if through the offence of one many be dead, much more the grace of God, and the gift by grace, which is by one man, Jesus Christ, hath abounded unto many" (Rom. 5:14–15). "And so it is written,

The first man Adam was made a living soul; the last Adam was made a quickening spirit" (1 Cor. 15:45).

So this is how our sins can be reckoned to Christ, and why Christ's righteousness can be reckoned to me. This is the gospel. This is how we are saved. The blood that Christ shed for us was the blood of the new *covenant*.

APPLICATION TO MARRIAGE

In all the counseling I have done, I have found that a misunderstanding of federal headship causes *many* of the difficulties in marriage. We do not think about marriage biblically because we do not think biblically about the covenant. Paul tells husbands to love their wives just as Christ loved the Church and gave Himself up for her as her representative head. Husbands therefore need to understand what Jesus did for His bride, and then do that for their wives. Before we can imitate Jesus, we have to understand what He did for us.

This is also tied in with our messed-up theology of how sinners come to God. There is a Christian song that goes, "Softly and tenderly Jesus is calling, calling for you and for me, see on the portals He's waiting and watching, watching for you and for me: 'Come home, come home, ye who are weary come home.'" In this view, Jesus is standing by the door of Heaven, wringing

His hands like that poor sap in high school who never could get a date, pleading with people to come because unless they choose to come He cannot save them. Some Christian husbands think that this is what Jesus did, and this is why we have a bunch of milksops for Christian husbands—*that* is what they are imitating.

But Jesus is the dragonslayer. Jesus is the one who came into this world to secure the salvation of His bride. When He went to the cross, He did not *try* to save anybody. When Jesus died on the cross, He was *settling* your salvation. You were bought and purchased when He died on the cross, and He is taking you home. If He died for you, there is no way you are not going to Heaven. This is the kind of efficacious love that husbands are called to imitate.

Husbands are not to be the autonomous boss-man of their homes. Being the head of the home does not mean being the loudest in the home. The husband is the true authority in the home, of course, but what is the *nature* of biblical authority? Being the head of the home does not mean being the most irritable one in the home. Being head of the home does not mean that you get your way all the time. We must be free from all individualism in marriage. We do not have two separated individuals, one of them arbitrarily granted tie-breaking authority. Rather, we have an organic covenantal *union* between a man and a woman, and so the foolishness of machismo is thus inconsistent with covenantal thinking. But rejecting machismo is not the same thing as diluting a husband's authority. Christ did not bully His disciples, but rather He washed their feet. But, having said this, He was also clearly and plainly their master and Lord (John 13:13).

So when husbands get a glimpse of what it means to be a head, it ought to scare them sideways. Headship does not mean that the husband gets his way in all the petty things. It does means that the husband cannot blame his wife for the state of their marriage. Just as Christ assumed responsibility for things He did not do, in the same way husbands should be willing to take responsibility for things their wives do.

Often I come into the counseling situation and the husband thinks, "We're all sinners, and my wife has contributed her share and I have contributed my share, and we need to meet in the middle." Now, there *are* sins that both parties have committed, but before we talk about any particular sins, I always make it clear to the couple that I consider 100 percent of the marriage's problems to be the husband's responsibility. The husband is the head, and so he is therefore responsible.

Husbands often do not like taking responsibility for things they did do, and so if you start asking them to take responsibility for things that they did *not* do, it shocks them. This is the single most difficult thing

I have to get across to men whose marriages are in trouble. When men fail to get this, they are failing to see what Jesus actually did. Jesus took responsibility for sins He did not commit. That is what the cross is. Paul says, "For he hath made him to be sin for us, who knew no sin; that we might be made the righteousness of God in him" (2 Cor. 5:21).

So if a man blames his wife for doing something he told her not to do, we should all remember that this is how the first Adam represented us. Adam told God in the Garden, "The woman whom thou gavest to be with me, she gave me of the tree, and I did eat" (Gen. 3:12). Husbands have been doing this from the beginning, right down to the present.

My father taught me many years ago that to find out why two kids are in a fight, you just ask each of them to tell you what the other one did. Then you will know the whole story, and probably quite a bit extra. Men do not like taking responsibility, especially for things they did not do. But that is what the gospel is: husbands, love your wives *as Christ loved the Church*.

Women are individuals who stand before God in their own right, and they must confess their particular sins to God. However, they are not responsible for the family as a whole in the same way their husbands are, and it is a sad fact that many husbands are not willing to take on this responsibility. But Scripture teaches that authority flows to those who take responsibility. This is why Jesus says that if you want to become great, then you need to become a servant. If you engage in blame-shifting, authority gathers up her skirts and runs away from you. The reason many husbands do not have authority in their own home is because they do not take responsibility there. If a man has a deeply embedded problem in his family, he should not go and blame his family for the problem. Instead, he should talk to God about it and take responsibility for the condition of the family in his prayers. He needs to start representing his family to God. He should come before God in prayer and say, "Father, *we* are a mess . . ." He must not begin with "Father, *they* . . ."

Within the covenant, love bestows loveliness. Out in the world, pagan men will say, "I love you because you are beautiful." The subtext is "and I will continue to love you as long as you continue to be beautiful." This is anti-covenantal thinking. The world tells us that wives are responsible to keep their husbands around, with *Cosmopolitan* magazine offering tips and tricks to help them do so. But the task is hopeless because now they are competing with all the young women out there. The wife turns forty, and all the twenty-five-year-olds are twenty-five. Ten years later, the twenty-five-year-olds are holding steady, still right there at twenty-five, and she, right on schedule, is now twice their age.

However, in our redemption, it is the love bestowed on us that makes us lovely. Romans 5:8 says, "But God commendeth his love toward us, in that, while we were yet sinners, Christ died for us." It is God's love of the unlovely that secured their loveliness. And the more a wife is loved in this way, the lovelier she grows.

This does not just mean that husbands should love their wives "a lot" because Christ loved the Church "a lot." Christ's love includes this of course, but the important thing about Christ's love is that it is a love that takes responsibility and *thereby* secures the loveliness of the beloved. If you want to know whether a husband is loving his wife, take a look at her ten or twenty years after they have been married. What is his love doing to her? Is it taking a toll on her or making her go to pieces? But love bestows loveliness. Ephesians 5:26–27 says Christ died for the Church "that he might sanctify and cleanse it with the washing of water by the word, that he might present it to himself a glorious church, not having spot, or wrinkle, or any such thing; but that it should be holy and without blemish."

This does not turn women into passive and inert objects. They are people who have their own relationship with God, and they are called by God to walk with Him as saints and Christians. But the two sexes nevertheless are created to function differently: men initiate, women respond; men sacrifice, women receive the sacrifice; men are to give their love, women are to grow in loveliness. A saintly woman is not the same thing as a saintly man.

EFFICACIOUS LOVE

If husbands and fathers learn to think of themselves as covenantal representatives, then they cannot go off into the back room in order to use pornography without it affecting the rest of the household. Every time he goes into your back room, he should think, "We, all of us, are going into this room, and I am bringing my wife and children together with me." The father is going there as the representative of the whole family.

A husband's love for his wife should be efficacious. Many husbands think they are loving their wives by criticizing them all the time, but this is not efficacious at all. That is just a critical eye and a critical spirit. Notice that when Christ efficaciously loved His bride, His love transformed her.

His love was also incarnational: Christ's love for the Church was embodied in His willingness to die for her. The first part of this is generally understood. A husband should be willing to die for his wife if an attacker breaks into their home, or if a mugger on the street attacks her. But a husband also needs to die daily for his wife, and the only way he will be able to do this is if he learns to take responsibility for things he did not do.

If I am walking by a softball field and I see the right fielder drop an easy fly ball and the shortstop is saying, "We can shake this off! We can do better!" then we know who the captain of the team probably is. The shortstop is taking responsibility for the balls he did not drop—and that is what Christian leadership looks like. But if you have a shortstop who yells and screams at the right fielder about what an idiot he is, I can tell you ahead of time which team is going to lose. That team has now given up playing against the opposite team, and they are now playing against each other.

I have yet to see a husband who takes godly responsibility for his wife and then whose wife takes ungodly advantage of it. I am sure it has happened sometime, but I haven't seen it yet. Wives are built by God to be responsive. This is because, as Paul says, "He that loveth his wife loveth himself" (Eph. 5:28). As a general rule, a husband who loves his wife is not loving someone eager to take advantage of him: women are built to respond in love. It is amazing to me how much some wives can love with how little encouragement they get. But when a husband really loves his wife, he will discover that as he gives these blessings to his wife, his wife consistently gives a bigger return. He shovels blessings on her, and then discovers that she has a much bigger shovel. He who loves his wife loves himself. She is always able to return more in blessing to him than he has given to her. Godly wives are multipliers.

Husbands who love their wives in an incarnational way will consequently have the authority to speak at the dinner table, and they will find that people want to listen. If a husband is not doing this, everyone around him will check out, right after they roll their eyes. If you are not loving your wife efficaciously, any instruction or teaching you offer your family is going to bounce off their foreheads. And if you want to transform your family, then you must be willing to die—and you cannot do this on your own. You have to look to the Christ who died, in order to imitate Him, daily taking up your cross and following Him.

CHAPTER 2

Common Sins in Marriage

Wherefore lay apart all filthiness and superfluity of naughtiness, and receive with meekness the engrafted word, which is able to save your souls. But be ye doers of the word, and not hearers only, deceiving your own selves. For if any be a hearer of the word, and not a doer, he is like unto a man beholding his natural face in a glass: for he beholdeth himself, and goeth his way, and straightway forgetteth what manner of man he was. But whoso looketh into the perfect law of liberty, and continueth therein, he being not a forgetful hearer, but a doer of the work, this man shall be blessed in his deed. If any man among you seem to be religious, and bridleth not his tongue, but deceiveth his own heart, this man's religion is vain. Pure religion and undefiled before God and the Father is this, to visit the fatherless and widows in their affliction, and to keep himself unspotted from the world. (Jas. 1:21–27)

The reason why I have begun a chapter on common sins in marriage with this passage is because it is all about what it means to be a Christian. The reason we want to be Bible-saturated Christians is because we want to check ourselves in that mirror regularly. We often are so close to situations that we cannot see ourselves accurately, and the fact that we are alone with our own thoughts and motives does not mean we understand them. As James tells us here, the Word of God is a *mirror*. Alone, we have trouble seeing the backs of our own heads. We need to look in the mirror of the Word and make sure that when we see ourselves, we do not forget what we looked like, trying to move on as quickly as we can.

SINS OF MEN

1. Abdication

I am going to discuss seven sins that husbands tend to commit and then move on to seven sins wives tend to commit. This will be done in a most evenhanded way, and with one eye on the text.

But the first and most fundamental sin that a man commits is forgetting that he is responsible for all of them. If we are talking about Bob and Suzie Smith, Bob is responsible for Bob's sins, Suzy is responsible for Suzy's sins, and Bob is responsible for all the Smiths' sins. The man is the head, whether he wants to be or not, and the only choice is whether he will be a good head or a bad head. He cannot *not* be a head. Even if the man abandons his family and flies to the other end of the country, his empty chair still dominates the table. He is still teaching about what headship is, but his abdication means he is teaching a lie about it. A husband does not have the option of being silent about Christ and the Church. All day, every day, in every word, a husband is teaching about Jesus. What he is living out is either true or false, but he is always teaching—when a father chooses to be absent, distant, grasping, or selfish, he is teaching his family lies.

This doctrine of corporate headship is hard for individualistic Americans to grasp or understand, let alone accept. In modern marriages, men and women are so mixed up and muddled on this particular point that they have *no idea what a public person is*. Remember what Paul says on this topic: "But I would have you know, that the head of every man is Christ; and the head of

the woman is the man; and the head of Christ is God"
(1 Cor. 11:3). If you are a Christian, you are obligated
to know what it means for Christ to be the head of
man, for God to be the head of Christ, and for the man
to be the head of the woman. What on earth is that
supposed to *mean*?

Many couples come to marriage counseling ses-
sions and assume that each party is responsible for
their own sins, whatever they are, and that the job
of the counselor is to help them meet in the middle.
There is a sense in which this does happen, but there
is a foundational covenantal sense in which it does not
happen at all. And so this is probably the most fundamental sin that men tend to commit: they abdicate
their federal responsibility.

2. Excuses, Excuses, Excuses

Men often refuse to be masculine. Paul says this:
"Watch ye, stand fast in the faith, quit you like men, be
strong" (2 Cor. 16:13). Men need to learn to be men.
If men are generally lacking in masculine initiative,
authority, and glad acceptance of sacrificial responsibility, then they will certainly lack it in their marriages.
Single men should know that marriage does not alter
what they are: it amplifies what they are. You might
think you are a selfless person only because you are living by yourself in an apartment, not getting in fights

with anybody. But if you get married, your latent self-ishness gets plugged into an amp and the volume is turned all the way up to eleven.

Many men come into marriage with all kinds of male desires, but without a sense of what real mascu-linity is. And so the sin that men need to avoid above all is the sin of making excuses. This is particularly important for young boys to learn. If they are making excuses for not getting their homework done, or for dropping the football, or for failing to complete their chores, then they are learning early on how to avoid and evade responsibility. And so young men need to learn how to avoid making excuses—even if they have a *good* excuse. This is because nine times out of ten they do not actually have a good excuse, and they need to practice not making them. Men who make excuses for the state of their marriage are not behav-ing like men.

3. Marital Infidelity

Jesus's words on this subject are well known, and their spirit is frequently disregarded: "Ye have heard that it was said by them of old time, Thou shalt not commit adultery: But I say unto you, That whosoever looketh on a woman to lust after her hath committed adultery with her already in his heart" (Matt. 5:27–28). This kind of lust is not the same thing as adultery in the eyes of the law: if a man commits adultery, his wife can legitimately divorce him. But while lust is the same as adultery in the eyes of God—the one who alone can see the heart—it is not grounds for divorce.

God sees everything that a man toys with or takes into his mind and heart. Many men sin against their wives by tolerating small compromises because they tell themselves that it will never go any farther and that consequently it will never destroy their marriage. That is like being a little bit pregnant: little sins always grow. If you tolerate it at all, it will demand more. Christian men are often unfaithful in their thoughts, whether provoked by magazines, coworkers, wives of friends, internet images, movies, or daydreams. Whatever it is, Jesus forbids it. Men are to be faithful to their wives, and this is because Christ is faithful to His bride, the Church.

4. Harsh Bitterness

Paul says this: "Husbands, love your wives, and be not bitter against them" (Col. 3:19). When men are bitter against someone, it comes out in a harsh and angry way. Men are very good at the blame game. Many husbands will blame things like their lust or marital infidelity on their wife's lack of sexual responsiveness. This is because they have become embittered at things their wife has done. Paul is warning against taking up a list of grievances and then using that as an excuse to lash out. Husbands do not have the right to excuse their behavior because of what their wives do or do not do.

5. Blockheadedness

What do I mean by being a blockhead? 1 Peter 3:7 says, "Husbands, likewise, dwell with them *with understanding*, giving honor to the wife, as to the weaker vessel, and as being heirs together of the grace of life, that your prayers may not be hindered" (NKJV). I want to focus on the phrase "dwell with them with understanding." Women are complicated beings, and Peter requires husbands to *study* them. The Word of God requires husbands to think through the ramifications of the things they see and do. A man cannot say that he has been a bachelor for a number of years and pretend that his inability to deal with women is therefore a permanent condition. After decades of life together she is still going to surprise you, and of course you will surprise her all the time. She is going to surprise you because different things always come out, and you surprise her because the same thing always comes out.

When men are redeemed by the blood of Christ, they are required by the Word of God to dwell with their wives "with knowledge." This means they need to be *intelligent* when it comes to their wives' responses. The Word of God does not permit a man to say that he did not know she felt that way. If you are not working on understanding how she feels, then the disobedience is yours, not hers.

6. Poor Provision

Paul says, "But if any provide not for his own, and specially for those of his own house, he hath denied the faith, and is worse than an infidel" (1 Tim. 5:8). A man is responsible to provide for his family before the Lord. A man cannot blame his boss or his circumstances for his failure at work. The Bible says that men are to provide for their own, period, and there is no excuse for not providing for their needs. If men do not do this, it is tantamount to apostasy.

This teaching may seem hard and cold, and as though it does not take into account the unpredictability of life. However, the Greek word for "provide" here means "to see beforehand." The job of providing entails looking down the road and anticipating what might happen; you do not want to be in a position where things are going fine one day and then the next there is a huge hospital bill or a broken-down car that you cannot pay for. Unexpected things happen all the time—some men anticipate it beforehand, and others do not. The people who do not see it coming are men who do not provide for their households. We do understand that there are times when enormously terrible disasters happen without the husband being at fault, and in such cases the Church should rally around and help people who are caught in circumstances beyond their control. So even when there is a genuine hard providence, the husband should take responsibility. But most of the time the problems that we have are of our own devising.

7. Laziness

Men must not be given to laziness. Man was created for work before the fall, and implicit in the command to keep the Sabbath on one day is the command to work for six. Many boys right now are learning the habits that will result in horrible things for their family and children twenty years down the road. Whether the habits are mental laziness, or laziness with regard to stacking the wood or taking out the garbage, such a boy is learning the way of poverty.

"He becometh poor that dealeth with a slack hand: but the hand of the diligent maketh rich" (Prov. 10:4). If a man has a slack hand and becomes poor because of it, that poverty is always visited upon his *household*. That is the way the world works. Husbands need to work hard and be more industrious than they are. Even when a good excuse comes up, assume masculine responsibility for all of your work. This is because lazy men make other people poor.

SINS OF WOMEN

1. Disrespect

Paul says, "Nevertheless let every one of you in particular so love his wife even as himself; and the wife see that she reverence her husband" (Eph. 5:33). Many women believe and understand that a husband is to love his wife unconditionally, but then they have a really hard time respecting unconditionally. The Bible does not say that husbands should love their wives *if* they are lovely, and it does not say wives should respect their husbands *if* they are respectable.

In particular, single ladies should not even dream of marrying a man they do not respect, because once they are married, it is their obligation to respect him—whether or not he is respectable. Your husband probably does fall short in many places that you are correct in noticing, but you must respect him anyway. Our generation talks a lot about unconditional love for wives, but almost no one talks about unconditional respect for husbands.

The biggest buyers of Christian marriage books are women, not men. It is the women who take them home, read them, and leave them around the house for their husband to perhaps notice, but he never takes the hint. Women often read those books, including books like this one, doing so because of their resentments against their husbands. Not only does it tell them all sorts of things that their husbands are not doing, but to add insult to injury their husbands are also refusing to read the book about it.

Paul says that love does not keep a record of wrongs (1 Cor. 13:5, NIV). If your marriage books are a scrapbook record of his wrongs, then throw them away. The husband must do what God tells him to do: his wife is not to give him a list of all his sins. If marriage books are causing a wife to disrespect her husband, she should throw them away and begin honoring him the way God says to honor him.

2. Resentment

Peter says, "Likewise, ye husbands, dwell with them according to knowledge, giving honour unto the wife, as unto the weaker vessel, and as being heirs together of the grace of life; that your prayers be not hindered" (1 Pet. 3:7). Peter does not explain what kind of weakness he is talking about here: it could be simply physical, or it could refer to emotional sensitivity.

However, some people infer wrongly that this means if the woman is hurt or offended by something the husband has done, she has a right to be offended. However, the Bible teaches that to be offended is as sinful as to give offense. Often people give offense simply because they are not thinking, but the person offended nurtures and builds up the offense over a period of years—making that a *deliberate* sin. That nursing of resentment is an offense against God, even if there was a real offense that started it all.

Paul says, "Let all bitterness, and wrath, and anger, and clamour, and evil speaking, be put away from you, with all malice" (Eph. 4:31). There are two types of people in the world, offenders and the offended, and often they are men and women, respectively. Men are thoughtless, and women take offense at all that thoughtlessness. We are to be tender and forgiving of one another, and this tenderness *must run in both directions*. If a husband has sinned against his wife, it is quite possible he has not sinned against her as much as she has sinned against him by taking offense. As God has forgiven all our sins for Jesus's sake, wives should be prepared to forgive theirs husbands, letting love overlook it. Be kind and tender-hearted as he learns to seek forgiveness.

Men tend towards a harsh bitterness; women tend towards resentful bitterness. Men need to apologize and seek forgiveness; women should drop it.

3. A Spirit of Accusation

Job 2:7–10 says this: "So went Satan forth from the presence of the Lord, and smote Job with sore boils from the sole of his foot unto his crown. And he took him a potsherd to scrape himself withal; and he sat down among the ashes. Then said his wife unto him, Dost thou still retain thine integrity? curse God, and die. But he said unto her, Thou speakest as one of the foolish women speaketh. What? shall we receive good at the hand of God, and shall we not receive evil? In all this did not Job sin with his lips."

There is a kind of theology that fashions God after our own likeness and says that God must only do happy things and that He must not create calamity. However, the Bible is clear that all calamity is from the Lord: "Shall a trumpet be blown in the city, and the people not be afraid? shall there be evil in a city, and the Lord hath not done it?" (Amos 3:6). Some people want just a happy face for God, a God who only creates kittens and pussy willows, and not a God who dwells in unapproachable light, terrible in His majesty. This is the god of the foolish women that Job speaks about.

Often men struggle under manifold temptations for an awful day, and then when they come through the door at the last part of the day, they find their wives waiting to jump on the dogpile. Often the men resist temptation until they get home, when their wives offer them yet one more occasion for sin, and so they lose it. Women are like Job's wife here, failing to minister to their husbands in light of the situation.

4. Little Helper Syndrome

It says in Proverbs that the foolish woman tears down her house with her own hands. Women can do this to their families, and like Job's wife, they can do so with their tongues. Paul says, "Neither was the man created for the woman; but the woman for the man" (1 Cor. 11:9). Wives are given to their husbands to be a *help*, not to be the Holy Spirit's little helper. The husband is not the woman's remodel project.

When a marriage is functioning the way it ought to function, the husband will seek his wife's input and she will have an opportunity to offer advice without being disrespectful. But if the husband does not ask for advice, this is where many women just decide to nag and badger him again and again to make sure he gets the message. But women do not wake up one morning and decide to drive their husbands crazy. They *think* they are helping their husbands, but they are in fact driving them up the wall. If you are guilty of nagging your husband, confess it as a sin and stop it.

5. Lack of Sexual Protection

Paul says, "Nevertheless, to avoid fornication, let every man have his own wife, and let every woman have her own husband" (1 Cor. 7:2). Paul teaches us here that one of the purposes of marriage is to provide protection against the many temptations to sexual immorality that exist out in the world. Not only are there Christian wives who are not a help to their husbands in this area, but there are some who are quite a stumbling block.

A wife is given to a man as a protection against sexual immorality. Now, appropriate sexual responsiveness is not to be defined by our sex-crazed culture, but neither is it to be defined by an uptight fundamentalist childhood. There are many women who think of marriage in a very sentimental, romantic way, and they go into marriage not expecting to be approached sexually very often. However, the essence of marriage is a covenant union that surrounds a sexual relationship.

A husband's duty is to be above board in his mental fidelity. He is responsible for his eyes, regardless of the responsiveness of his wife, period. However, the model for Christian wives is neither the Victorians nor the faces and bodies found in all the women's magazines. The model is the Shulamite in the Song of Songs.

6. False Submissiveness

Paul says that wives are to submit to their husbands as the Church submits to Christ (Eph. 5:22), but many women do not understand what submission actually is. They are tired of bearing the weight of decision-making, and they think that they want the husband to take initiative. But what they really want is for the husband to do what they were doing for him, and without him making any decisions they disagree with. They want to back off leading in the home, but they still want him to make the decisions they were making when they were still running everything.

Wives are not really submitting when their husbands are doing things they agree with. When he takes you out on a date to your favorite restaurant, you are not really submitting to him in your willingness to go. If your husband comes to a decision that you do not agree with and you think he is being foolish, even though it is possible that he is making a bad decision, this is where submission is to be exercised.

Many women want their husbands to *look* like they are leading, but they do not want them to actually lead. They want the neighbors and other folks to see a good show, and they want the honors that go with it, but they are not willing to pay the cost. A godly husband will take responsibility and he will seek his wife's counsel, but this does not mean that he should do everything she likes.

7. *A Leaky Faucet*

Proverbs 19:13 notes that "a foolish son is the calamity of his father: and the contentions of a wife are a continual dropping." The Word of God says that a wife who will not let things go and keeps on airing her concerns is like a leaky faucet. Many women say that they just want to have their husbands hear their point of view just one more time, simply to make sure they were heard.

None of this means that you cannot have back-and-forth discussions where husband and wife talk it out. You can even have a genuine disagreement, and the husband should be able to repeat back a wife's position. In such cases, the wife can feel like she was heard.

However, if a wife is having difficulty in her marriage, she should not wait for her husband to fix it all. She cannot control his obedience, so she should start by obeying herself. Chances are, if the wife keeps pushing for her side and her husband is not responding to her, then he turned her off a long time ago. He does not know how to fix that particular problem, and so he tunes her out. This is a sinful, abdicating response on his part, but a wife *can* reduce the temptation she is putting on her husband. She can do this by backing off her attempts to "be heard" constantly.

CHAPTER 3

The Sketch of a Godly Husband

According to the doctrine of federal headship, the husband is the head of the wife in an analogous way that Christ is the head of the Church. The Bible does not say that husbands ought to be the head in their home: it says that the husband already *is* the head of the home. The only question is whether he is going to be a poor head or a godly head. In this chapter, I want to provide a sketch of a godly husband, and I want to consider this verse: "A virtuous woman is a crown to her husband: but she that maketh ashamed is as rottenness in his bones" (Prov. 12:4).

If the wife is a crown, then the husband is a king, which means that the husband and wife should fit each other. You do not want an ornate crown on a tiny head, and you do not want a plastic crown on a great king. This is why if you are looking for someone to marry, you need to become the kind of person that the kind of person you would want to marry would want to marry. In this chapter I am going to focus on the kind of man who would be adorned and complemented by such a crown.

A MAN'S CALIBER

Our notion of what a godly husband ought to be should not be based on a particular set of cultural assumptions or a particular personality type that our culture happens to approve of currently. We always should take our questions to Scripture and have it provide us with an understanding of what godliness is.

A godly husband should love Jesus Christ more than anything or anyone. Jesus says this in Luke 14:26: "If any man come to me, and hate not his father, and mother, and wife, and children, and brethren, and sisters, yea, and his own life also, he cannot be my disciple." Now here Jesus is using hyperbole: He is not saying that we should go around filled with malicious spite toward father and mother, wife and children. The

Bible says elsewhere to honor our father and mother and to love our wives (cf. Exod. 20:12; Matt. 15:4–6; Eph. 5). In the parallel passage in Matthew, Jesus makes the same point a little differently: "He that loveth father or mother *more than me* is not worthy of me: and he that loveth son or daughter *more than me* is not worthy of me" (10:37, emphasis added). Jesus is saying that we should love Him with everything we have, so that all our other loves pale in comparison. Therefore, a Christian husband must be a Christian who is completely dedicated to the glory of God through Jesus Christ.

When a man loves Christ more than anything else and his wife is number two, she receives far more attention and love as number two than if she were number one. Because he is an idolater, a man who worships his wife has cut himself off from the source of all love. He is going to run out of strength very quickly, but if he loves Christ the way the Bible says to, then he will have the strength to love her as Christ loved the Church. If your one central goal in life is to keep your wife happy, then the one thing I can guarantee is that you are not going to make her happy.

When Jesus Christ tells us to disciple the nations, He does not say to baptize them and teach them to be middle class and respectable. He says that we are to "teach them to obey all the things I have commanded them" (Matt. 28:20). A Christian husband must be a *Christian*.

He must love God, and he cannot love God unless his heart is transformed and he has been born again.

True godliness is not measured by church attendance or doing normal middle-class, respectable things. It is measured by whether the husband honestly loves Jesus Christ. If someone puts a gun to your head and tells you to deny Jesus, you must say *no* because you love Him. If you cannot do this, then that is the problem with your family.

THE WAY A MAN STANDS

A godly Christian husband must be a man, not a boy. Nehemiah 4:14 says, "And I looked, and rose up, and said unto the nobles, and to the rulers, and to the rest of the people, Be not ye afraid of them: remember the Lord, which is great and terrible, and fight for your brethren, your sons, and your daughters, your wives, and your houses." In the book of Numbers, the age required for going to war is twenty (1:2–3). Before that, a boy was not qualified to be considered an independent warrior who could fight for his family. Unlike the modern practice of conscription where we basically kidnap people, Israelites were required to volunteer for war. You would show up, and if you were cowardly or had just gotten married, you were released and sent home (Deut. 20:5–8). No one was forced into battle at gunpoint, but everyone had the responsibility to assemble, and everyone had to decide whether to man up or not. The nation could require you to muster but could not lawfully require you to go to war.

Notice that I just used the phrase "man up." When I say a godly husband should be a man, not a boy, we are not talking merely about size and height. There are many husbands who are simply boys who shave and have a job. True masculinity entails the taking of responsibility, as well as physical maturity. Part of the reason many husbands do not have this maturity is because we live in an era that is deeply hostile to the idea of biblical masculinity, even among Christians. If I tell people to "man up" or use that word *manly*, the first thing that will pop into your head is some guy pounding on his chest like Tarzan. It is extremely easy to make fun of masculinity in times of peace and prosperity. However, when there is a hot war at the city gates, manliness is something that is prized and recognized as necessary for survival.

In a church where marriage is valued, the boys should want to be married before they are ready to be married. When you see little boys playing at war and little girls playing house, the feminist movement catechizes you to think that this is something that society is imposing on them. However, what is happening is that the little kids look at the adults and they want to grow up to be like them. Young boys should want to grow up to be like their dad, and little girls should want to grow up to be like their mom. If the boys are not training to become men, when they grow up, they are not going to know how to be men. Parents need to honor this process and ought to make plenty of room for it.

So a husband must cultivate his sense of responsibility and masculinity. That does not mean that every single cultural assignment of particular duties for men and others for women applies to all times and places. Different cultures have different ways of displaying manliness and femininity. However, there are certain aspects of it that are built into the created order, and this includes men fighting for their families.

So even though things like men taking out the trash may not be a law for every culture, we should honor customs that are culturally assigned to the two genders. The Bible says that we are to show honor to those to whom honor is due (Rom. 13:7). In the American military you show honor by saluting your superior officer with the palm facing down, while in the British military you show honor by saluting with the palm facing out. The Bible does not say which way to salute, but both are signs of honor, and every culture needs particular ways of showing honor. One way husbands can take responsibility for their family is by opening the car door for their wives. There is nothing in the Bible that says the husband should open the car door for his wife, but we need to have particular ways of communicating to our wives, to our children, and to the watching world that we take seriously the responsibilities that God has assigned us.

VOCATION

Third, a man should be prepared for his vocation. Paul says in 1 Corinthians 11:8–9, "For the man is not of the woman: but the woman of the man. Neither was the man created for the woman; but the woman for the man." A man not prepared for vocation is not prepared for marriage. As I often tell young men, women are expensive. This does not mean that a young husband needs to be in his final occupation before he marries, but he does need to have a sense of purpose, direction, and calling. A man in his second year of med school doesn't have his practice yet, but he does have his direction.

God created Adam and gave him the task of naming the animals and exercising dominion over the world. It was in that setting that God said it was not good for man to be alone, and He made Eve as a helper suitable for him. That is what Paul is alluding to in this passage: the woman was given to the man to help him fulfill his vocation. When a man is preparing for marriage, he needs to know that the woman is coming to help him fulfill his calling in the world. This means that he should have some sense about what his calling is. This does not mean a man cannot change jobs, but if a young man is going to college and is changing his major every year without any idea of how to pay the bills, then he is not ready for marriage. He should have a good sense of where he is headed, and he should seek a woman who will help him fulfill that vocation.

This is why a couple of teenagers should not pair off, and this is because they are not grown up. The young man especially needs to grow up first, and he should not bypass the ten years of maturation that are necessary for stepping into this role. The young man should come into marriage understanding what marriage is, the nature of the vows he is taking, and his duty to love his wife in the same way as Christ loved the Church. A man should enter into his marriage expecting to exercise leadership and knowing how to make a decision.

LEADERSHIP

Leadership is not being bombastic or dogmatic. It is not coming home and demanding everything your way. Leadership includes being like Jesus when He got down and washed the disciples' feet. But it also includes being like Jesus when He rebuked His disciples for squabbling about who was the greatest. When husbands sacrifice the way God wants them to, that is the foundation of all authority. Biblical Christian leadership is built on the foundation of men giving themselves up for the sake of their families.

Leadership does not mean yelling. Leadership does not mean losing your temper. Leadership means a pattern of sacrifice such that when you make a decision, everybody *wants* to go where you lead. This is not the same thing as the feminist understanding of marriage, where the wife's perspective is always right and the husband is a doormat. So if you think that sacrificial leadership is just letting your wife have her way, then you are actually abdicating. It is sacrifice that enables the family to want to follow you, because they know that you have their best interests in mind. When godly husbands sacrifice and bleed, their wives *want* to obey them and follow them because they know the husband is being a sacrificial man, which is to say, a masculine man.

How can a man be ready for this? The only way to get ready is to realize that no one is ready. Paul illustrated this principle in a different area when he asked, "And who is sufficient for these things?" (2 Cor. 2:16). The implied answer is that no one is sufficient for these things but Christ. We have no sufficiency in ourselves, but we know that by the grace of God a godly husband can assume masculine responsibility for his family.

MONOGAMY

A godly husband is monogamous to the bone. At the creation, God said that it was not good for man to be alone, and when God decided to remedy this, He did not give Adam a harem, another man, or one of the animals. God's pattern is one woman, one time. Centuries later, Jesus pointed back to this example as authoritative: "And he answered and said unto them, Have ye not read, that he which made them at the beginning made them male and female, and said, For this cause shall a man leave father and mother, and shall cleave to his wife: and they twain shall be one flesh? Wherefore they are no more twain, but one flesh. What therefore God hath joined together, let not man put asunder" (Matt. 19:4–6). Christians should want the creation design to be imitated and followed. Christ Himself is married to one woman, the Christian Church, and husbands are told to imitate this. This includes being as single-minded in his devotion to his wife as Christ is to the Church.

Furthermore, Paul requires that if a man wants to be an elder in the Church, he needs to be a one-woman man: "A bishop then must be blameless, the husband of one wife" (1 Tim. 3:2). The New Testament also says that elders are meant for everyone else to imitate: "Obey them that have the rule over you, and submit yourselves: for they watch for your souls, as they that must give account, that they may do it with joy, and not with grief: for that is unprofitable for you" (Heb. 13:17). In a world where polygamy was fairly common, Paul forbade having polygamous Church leaders. Our culture for the last thousand years has been monogamous because of the strong influence of the Christian gospel. Monogamy follows Christianity, and it does so for a reason.

Now, some Christians object to this because Abraham and David had multiple wives and because the Old Testament allowed for polygamy in certain situations. Now it is true that the Bible does allow it in certain situations. If a missionary goes to a tribe and a man with three wives is converted, that is not an ideal situation, but that man ought to start coming to church with his three wives. All of them should be baptized. In the law, a man who took a second wife was not allowed to divorce his first wife (Exod. 21:10). A polygamous man should be received into membership in a church, but he should be barred from leadership, according to Paul's instructions in 1 Timothy. I think that polygamy in the Old Testament was allowed in much the same way that divorce was allowed in cases of sexual immorality. Polygamous marriages are valid marriages, but they nevertheless fall short of God's creation design. Even in the Old Testament era they fell short of God's design. No one looks at the great baby race between

Jacob's wives and concubines and wishes that he could be in that position.

And so again, a godly Christian husband is to be monogamous to the bone. This excludes adultery, lust, flirtations, pornography, or snide, comparative comments ("Why can't you be more like her?"). This also excludes unbiblical divorce and remarriage, which is nothing more than serial polygamy. A Christian man is to be devoted to one woman. He should not want to be with any other woman, and he is to be faithful to his wife, period, end.

We continue to exist in a fallen world, and so wives should not be surprised or horrified at the mere fact of temptation. When a man accepts this biblical standard, as he must, he is walking up a steep incline. The whole world is against him, including the advertising industry, the internet, and the way women on the street and at his office are dressing. This means that a faithful husband needs to be disciplined and focused, but wives should not make the mistake of thinking that because the standard is required it should somehow be easy. We do not need to coddle men, "Oh, poor baby!" but wives do need to understand the obstacles the man is overcoming. If he is being faithful to her, she should be grateful and expect it, but she should also know the nature of the gift that is being given to her.

THE LOST VIRTUE OF TRIBALISM

A godly husband is tribal, which means he thinks in terms of his ancestors and his descendants. The first commandment promises blessings to a thousand generations: "Thou shalt not bow down thyself to them, nor serve them: for I the Lord thy God am a jealous God, visiting the iniquity of the fathers upon the children unto the third and fourth generation of them that hate me and shewing mercy unto thousands of them that love me, and keep my commandments" (Exod. 20:5–6). If people are faithful to God, then God gives mercy to them—to a thousand generations. Therefore, a godly husband thinks of his great-grandparents and of his great-grandchildren.

It says in 2 Chronicles 4:9–10, "And Jabez was more honourable than his brethren: and his mother called his name Jabez, saying, Because I bare him with sorrow. And Jabez called on the God of Israel, saying, Oh that thou wouldest bless me indeed, and enlarge my coast, and that thine hand might be with me, and that thou wouldest keep me from evil, that it may not grieve me! And God granted him that which he requested."

A godly man does not think in terms of raw accumulation. He is not trying to accumulate money or resources or houses or descendants so that he can have a big mound of riches that he can sit on top of and enjoy until he dies. A godly man should want more blessings for his family, for his children, for his grandchildren. He should want his boundaries enlarged because we cannot give away things that we do not have. We have a deep suspicion of accumulating wealth, but we should want to put seed in the ground so that we can gather a harvest. We give in order to get, in order that we might give again. God is constantly generous to us and overflows to us, and our duty as fathers and husbands is to be like Him, which means we must have stuff to give away. So when a man wants God to prosper his business, when he wants God to establish his family, when he wants his children to learn to work and thrive, those are all good things. When the children have a good reputation, God is enlarging a man's territory.

A godly husband is responsible for more than just having a lot of children. He is responsible for instructing and teaching them. After he has begotten them, he needs to feed them. He should not want to just do his job and pay the bills, and then retire for the last twenty years of his life, as though consumption were the chief end of man. He should want to work to bless his family, bless his business, and bless his territory. God is open-handed with us, and we should want to be open-handed with what He has given us.

A WORK ETHIC

A godly husband is industrious, and this standard of industry is not determined by the labor unions. We somehow got the idea that a forty-hour-workweek is something God handed down to Moses on Mount Sinai, but there is nothing inherently biblical about working forty hours a week. If your work dominates you, that is a problem; if your leisure time dominates you, that is a problem also. What a man should do is work hard in such a way that his wife and children appreciate it. The godly husband does not sit for endless hours at home, staring slack-jawed at the tube. Neither is he gone all the time, justifying it by saying he is providing for his household. He has a responsibility to provide money *and* to be a father and husband. He has to provide dinner, but he also has to provide a dad to be present there at the dinner.

Now there are times—if a man is a farmer, say—when during harvest season he must work extra hours, with the phrase "extra hours" being a gross understatement. This is fine for a season since the work eventually slows down, and life goes back to normal. However, if a husband is absent all the time, then he is failing to provide for his family all that his family really needs. A good husband spends time with his wife and children so that he can teach and encourage them, and play with them and enjoy them.

PROVIDER

A godly husband provides food and clothing. As we have noted already, in the Old Testament, God placed restrictions on polygamy. Polygamy was substandard, though tolerated in the Old Testament, and it was meant to be phased out. One of the ways the law discouraged polygamy was if a man took another wife, he was not allowed to diminish his first wife's food, clothing, or conjugal rights (Exod. 21:10). In ancient society, this baseline requirement would have discouraged men from taking a second wife. It would have discouraged polygamy as a form of "in-house divorce," where the first wife was neglected.

So even though this law was intended to discourage polygamy, we can see some of the essential duties of a husband in this passage. A husband's responsibility includes making sure his wife has a full closet, a full cupboard, and full arms. That is the baseline of what a husband owes to his wife. A husband should, of course, want to grow and surpass that, but he must not drop below this. He needs to provide his wife the wherewithal to buy clothes and food, and he needs to provide her with a warm, affectionate relationship.

This includes giving her a sexual relationship so that she can have children. This means a husband must be sexually attentive. We live in a fallen world, and both men and women need to be protected from straying; Paul says that because of sexual immorality, each man should have his own wife and each woman her own husband (1 Cor. 7:2). If a man does not have that covenantal center, the world will not hesitate to offer alternatives. For the godly man, this means listening to his wife and being thoughtful.

A WALL AROUND HIS WIFE

Finally, the husband needs to be courageous. In our nation, we have drifted into a state where we defend ourselves by sending eighteen-year-olds as cannon-fodder. However, in the Old Testament rules for warfare, heads of households were supposed to be represented there. While that means that there will be many household tragedies, it is part of the cost of having the kind of society where men protect their families and are willing to die for them.

A godly husband is someone who stands between his wife and the various blows and insults that come from the world. If something is said or done to his wife that is insulting or hurtful, he needs to speak to the person involved. A husband sometimes even has to protect his wife from other family members: things her parents or her in-laws might say to her might be very harmful, and in such cases the husband needs to step in and say, "No, you may not say that: I am my wife's protector now." A godly husband is a wall around his wife.

PUTTING IT ALL TOGETHER

Husbands should love Jesus Christ so that they can learn to become like Jesus Christ. There are husbands who think that biblical headship is a matter of yelling, browbeating, or bossing people around, and then they act surprised when nobody listens to them. If a husband is in this situation and sees it as his wife's problem or his kids' problem for not "obeying" him, then he needs to take a careful look in the mirror. His wife knows that he is being a selfish pig and that he is just adorning it with Bible verses. He needs to rethink his position.

Jesus says this: "The scribes and the Pharisees sit in Moses's seat: All therefore whatsoever they bid you observe, that observe and do; but do not ye after their works: for they say, and do not. For they bind heavy burdens and grievous to be borne, and lay them on men's shoulders; but they themselves will not move them with one of their fingers" (Matt. 23:2–4).

There are many husbands who lay heavy burdens on their wives, and then will not move a finger to help them. They ask their wives to do all sorts of things, many of which may be quite good in themselves. In the same way, many of the things the Pharisees commanded were good, and Jesus told His disciples to go ahead and do them. However, the problem was the pharisaical mind wants someone else to do the toting and fetching and carrying. For example, there are many men who want their wives to homeschool. Homeschooling is a wonderful and honorable thing to do, but a husband who does not help or take responsibility for this task is letting the full burden of the work fall on his wife. That is *no bueno*.

But when men exercise bleeding authority, then their wives and children know they have protective leadership that is watching out for them.

CHAPTER 4

The Sketch of a Godly Wife

When reading a book like this, it is important for the husband and wife not to give most of their attention to the duties being assigned to their spouse. Many husbands and wives make excuses by saying, "Well, until the other person starts doing what *they* ought to be doing, I do not need to do anything I am supposed to be doing either!"

This is not how the Word of God comes to us: it says husbands, love your wives as Christ loved the Church. It does not say love your wife *if* she respects you as she should. The Bible tells wives to respect their husbands. It does not say to respect him *if* he is respectable. If we understand the doctrine of federal headship, of course we understand that the husband is a public person responsible for the whole household. However, at the same time, each member of the household is responsible for their own individual sins. So consequently, wives should not think their husband is responsible for every single thing such that they cannot do anything until he gets his act together. It is true that as husbands obey God and submit to His Word, their wives' tasks will be made much simpler, but a wife's obligations do not disappear simply because of how much she thinks her husband is not doing.

A QUALIFICATION FIRST

Before I get into the particulars, I need to give a defense of even addressing wives and calling them to their duties. In the modern world, a particular type of exhortation has been placed off limits because of the feminist movement, and this has robbed Christian women of the right to hear the Word of God. This has happened by people claiming that any criticism of a particular woman is an assault on all women. This has had the effect of robbing Christian women of pastoral care.

For instance, suppose I were to address lazy housewives from the pulpit. Even assuming that there were only three of them in the entire state of Idaho, if I did this, there would immediately be an uproar: "Are you saying that women are lazy?" However, I would not be attacking *women* at all: I would be attacking a particular sin that some women are vulnerable to. To say that a particular class of people is vulnerable to a particular temptation is not to say that every member of that class of people has succumbed to that temptation.

When I exhort Christian husbands, I am pretty straightforward, and everyone in our circles generally agrees with what I am saying. If I say that the husband who does not provide for his wife is worse than an unbeliever, and someone were to object, saying, "My leg is broken and so I cannot work. How dare you say that I am worse than an unbeliever," we would know what the problem was. Exceptional cases make bad laws, and we do not adopt general expectations for a class of people based on those exceptions. Within the Church today we do not get that reaction when we are speaking to men. This is because the biblical teaching on federal headship can at first glance be confused with our generation's predisposition to male-bashing. However, if a preacher turns around and gives women the mildest of exhortations, people's feelings get hurt.

A TRUE HELP NEEDED

Many women tend to assume that their intentions are the measurement of their work. While it is wonderful that God has created women to be eager to help their men, we always need to define help, not according to the intentions but according to the Word of God. We might recall C.S. Lewis's line on this topic: "She's the sort of woman who lives for others—you can always tell the others by their hunted expression."[1]

That women stumble in this area should not be surprising. If women are created to be a help to their husbands, then we should expect them to stumble there, in the arena of helping. Scripture says that an excellent wife is the crown of her husband, while a bad one is rottenness in his bones. So, as a woman reads this, she should hear the Word of God and be ready for what God is saying to her through it. She should not go to her husband in a panic, asking whether she *really* is a help to him. If she is not helping him, and chances are that someone reading this book is not helping in some ways, then he might actually have something to criticize. However, since the wife is panicking, she will just melt down at what he says, and he will then be tempted to take what he said back and patch it all up. Then the two will stagger down the road for another couple of years.

Now obviously in such a case the husband is sinning by patching things up and the responsibility for *that* lies with him, but women should not try to manipulate their husbands with their tears. We need to go to

1.   C.S. Lewis, *The Screwtape Letters* (1942; New York: HarperCollins, 1996), 145.

the mirror of the Word of God; husbands should not look in the mirror of their wives, and wives should not look in the mirror of their husbands. So, she should ask God if she is doing what she ought to be doing and she should be ready for what she sees: the truth of Scripture cannot be manipulated by anyone's tears.

Men must repent as men of men's sins, and women must repent as women of women's sins. Men often want to repent on behalf of their wives and women want to repent on behalf of their husbands, but confessing someone else's sins will not cause your own joy to return. If a husband's sins are great and glaring and his wife concentrates on them, she can confess those sins all day and nothing will change. However, if she confesses her own sins *as though she were the only one in the relationship who sinned*, then she is doing it right.

This may not be a very sentimental approach to marriage, and it may seem very cold and hard, but it is the kind of coldness we need. We need a bracing word of truth, and we cannot go through life in a vast haze of sentiment without asking how the Word of God applies to our lives.

RESPECT

When we hold up the mirror of the Word, it says that a godly woman respects her husband: "Nevertheless let each one of you in particular so love his own wife as himself, and let the wife see that she respects her husband" (Eph. 5:33, NKJV). God does not tell wives to love their husbands, nor does He tell husbands to respect their wives. Of course, as Christians, we are all to love our neighbors, which would include husbands. However, Scripture commands to our weaknesses, and when it speaks to women *in their office* as wives, it tells them to respect their husbands. The one exception to this is Titus 2:3–5, where it says that the older women are to teach the younger women to be husband-lovers and children-lovers. I would describe this as "being into husbands and kids," and because of the context of the passage, I would interpret it as a command for women to be oriented towards the home. It is a command to be domestic.

Sometimes a woman is willing to consider marrying a man who is a real jerk, and when her friends ask her why she keeps going back to him, she will say it is because she *loves* him. However, if you were to ask her whether she respects him, she would probably laugh and say, "Him? Really?" However, a woman should not even think twice about marrying a man she does not respect. This is because Scripture commands wives to *respect* their husbands.

In Ephesians 5, men are told to love their wives. Naturally, husbands should respect their wives. Paul tells us to give honor to whom honor is due (Rom. 13:7), and so husbands need to honor their wives, just like they are to respect and honor their neighbors. However, when God speaks to men, He tells them to concentrate on loving their wives, and when He speaks to wives specifically, He says they are to respect and honor their husbands.

Women run on love, and men run on respect. Some cars run on diesel, and others use regular. Men and women function differently, and we should not try to fix things by giving the other person the thing we would like to get. Frequently, wives give their husbands what they would like to be getting. She shows him signs of her tenderness and thoughtfulness and expresses how much she loves him. However, this is not what God said she should make sure to render to her husband.

Suppose a wife wonders how she could ever possibly respect her husband—because, as it turns out, he is a bozo. However, if a husband said he cannot love his wife until she makes herself more lovely, we would know that the problem lies entirely with him—husbands should love their wives unconditionally. However, this also goes the other way: wives should not sit in judgment on their husbands and wait until he passes a test before she shows respect. She is required by God to respect him *now*.

There are many times that I have seen husbands fail in remarkable ways. I have seen marriages that are real trainwrecks, but even then, I have never seen a husband come into my office who was as depraved as it is possible for a human to be. I have met lousy husbands, but no orcs. There is always some little area where the wife could legitimately respect her husband for certain things he had accomplished. In the hard cases, she might itemize a list of things he has accomplished and ask the Lord to show her how to honor him more. Now, in some such situations, the duty may be simply to salute the uniform and respect the office that he holds, rather than the man himself. But for most Christian couples, however, there are a host of things that men do for their families that too often go unrecognized and unacknowledged. Ask God to reveal some of those.

When respect is not rendered, it is often in situations where it could easily be rendered, and pride is the only thing standing in the way. "I would feel dumb or awkward saying that, and he would say I was doing it because I read about it in a book." Well, worse things have happened than doing what was learned in a book.

HOUSE-DESPOT

A godly woman manages her home well. Again, remember what Paul commands wives to do: "The aged women likewise, that they be in behaviour as becometh holiness, not false accusers, not given to much wine, teachers of good things; that they may teach the young women to be sober, to love their husbands, to love their children, to be discreet, chaste, keepers at home, good, obedient to their own husbands, that the word of God be not blasphemed" (Titus 2:3–5). In Proverbs 31:27, it says that the wise woman "looketh well to the ways of her household, and eateth not the bread of idleness."

This is said because some women *do* eat the bread of idleness. Women are to be praised for cleaning up, cooking, preparing, providing, and doing all these things for their families because there are some women who do not do them. A godly wife has managerial responsibilities and must cultivate those skills: she is the executive officer of the home. The Greek word that means "keepers at home" above could also be translated "house-despot." So take off your shoes where she tells you to.

The husband is, of course, the head of the home, but he is not the head in such a way that she becomes a mere functionary. Scripture delegates the responsibility for running the home to her, and she should be industrious within this domain. Again, even though there are exceptional cases, I am trying here to describe the scriptural ideal. If something prevents us from doing our duty, such as an injury or other circumstances out of our control, we should ask God to help us get back to the point where we can start fulfilling our duties again.

It is often said that a woman's place is in the home. This does not mean that a woman cannot do things outside of the home, such as hospitality or volunteer work, but her primary responsibility is within the home. If someone were to repeat the old saying that a woman's place is in the home, I would want to say, with a glance at Proverbs 31, that a woman's *priority* should be the home.

THE TONGUE

A godly woman is in command of her tongue: "She openeth her mouth with wisdom; and in her tongue is the law of kindness" (Prov. 31:26).

Many women tear their homes apart with their carping, whining, complaining, resentful comments, and criticism. When those in a woman's household think of her words, does the phrase "law of kindness" come to mind? If it is not the first thing that pops into their minds, then the prayer should be that it would *become* the first thing they think of.

The Bible says it is better to live in the corner of an attic than with a woman who is constantly nagging (Prov. 21:9). A woman who nags is like a leaky faucet (Prov. 27:15). Do you see a law of kindness, or do you see accusations, frustration, whining, and complaining? James says that if someone is able to control their tongue, they are able to control everything (Jas. 3:2). This is therefore an important thing for wives to master—and is a key to getting the rest of the household under control as well.

A LOCKED GARDEN

A godly woman is sexually responsive: "I am my beloved's, and his desire is toward me" (Song of Sol. 7:1).

We often careen from one extreme to the other. Prudishness is not biblical, and Christians should be open about the fact that marriage relationships are publicly acknowledged sexual relationships. But some Christian women have inherited a Victorian mentality, and they take their stand in opposition to the licentiousness of our times. While it is good to be opposed to the pornography, immodesty, and general crassness of our time, the antidote should be *biblical* thinking and living. Hebrews 13:4 says, "Marriage is honourable in all, and the bed undefiled: but whoremongers and adulterers God will judge." God's law is hostile to all sexual misbehavior, but notice also that it says the marriage bed is to be honored among Christians. When a wedding happens, we should be clear in our minds about the sexual aspect of the marriage.

A woman should be a locked garden that no one can approach except her husband. She should not be dressing in such a way that acts as though others could walk right in—even if she actually would not let them in. On the other hand, she should not be a safe whose lock combination changes every other day, baffling her husband most of all. Some women are really difficult to approach sexually, and it tempts their husbands to wander. This does not give their husbands the *right* to wander, and he certainly should not use a book like this as a club to beat up his wife with. However, all of us have enough temptations on our hands without adding more to the pile.

PROVIDING FOR THE HOME

A godly woman shops wisely: "She is like the merchants' ships; she bringeth her food from afar" (Prov. 31:14). Shopping for groceries and clothing is not a woman's recreation: it is her vocational responsibility, and she must do it wisely and well.

This means that the woman's husband should provide her with the means to do her work well. He should not be like Pharaoh, telling her to make bricks without straw. As I mentioned in the previous chapter, a husband's duty is to keep his wife's closet full, her cupboard full, and her arms full. This does not mean that a woman has the right to be extravagant, or wild, or to run the family into financial troubles. However, if a woman shops wisely, she is doing the work God has called her to do. Some women are good at it, and others are wasteful. Those who are good at it should give pointers to the less experienced.

As children are brought up, boys are becoming men and girls are becoming women. Boys are becoming fathers, and girls are becoming mothers, yet many girls arrive at adulthood without having been taught how to do basic things like what used to be taught in home economics. This is where older men and older women in the body of Christ should teach the younger folks who do not know how to do these things.

Proverbs 31:5 says that "she riseth also while it is yet night, and giveth meat to her household, and a portion to her maidens." The godly woman anticipates the needs of the household. She provides, she is industrious as the executive of the home, and she knows of the need for good food. Far too many modern people eat their meals on their way out the door, or they microwave it and eat it leaning over the sink. But if you want to build a civilization, you need to have families that sit down at a table together. This means that there must be something on the table that makes it worth it, so a woman should study how to be skilled in how she makes the family meals.

Some of you may think this is straight out of the 1950s, but it is actually what the human race has been doing for a long, long time. We are living in a weird little historical bubble where we are trying to repeal the law of gravity. Men are supposed to bring home the bacon, and women are supposed to make it edible.

THEOLOGICALLY EDUCATED

A godly woman is to be theologically educated. Paul says, "Let the woman learn in silence with all subjection" (1 Tim. 2:11). While the woman is supposed to learn in quietness and submission, she still has to be *learning*. In conservative circles, we sometimes wrongly overemphasize the submission and conclude that women do not need to learn anything doctrinal at all, but this is not what Paul says here. Men and women are both to be disciples of Jesus, both are co-laborers in the gospel, and both explain theology, doctrine, and biblical history to their children. Women are as much part of the intellectual arm of the Christian faith as are the men.

It is true that women are not to teach or have authority over men, and are excluded from the elder board and from the pulpit by the Scriptures, but this does not mean that women can check out when it comes to doing theology. Both men and women together should understand their vocational pursuits in the light of the teaching of the Word of God, whether that involves engineering or the domestic pursuits. One of the lies of feminism is that the work of the home is unimportant and that what the men are doing "out in the world" is the important stuff. This kind of thinking sometimes seeps into the Church, and many Christians falsely think that the light of the Word of God does not need to be directed at the vocation of homemaking.

Incidentally, this means that husbands need to give their wives a chance to hear the sermon regularly. It is a challenge for little ones to sit through a service, and keeping order in the service is hard. Husbands should not be sitting and listening to the sermon at the time while their wives are trying to keep the troops in line. The husband and wife together should take turns keeping order, because both of them need to hear the Word of God.

LOVE OF LEADERSHIP

A godly woman respects masculine leadership. Paul says, "Let your women keep silence in the churches: for it is not permitted unto them to speak; but they are commanded to be under obedience as also saith the law. And if they will learn any thing, let them ask their husbands at home: for it is a shame for women to speak in the church" (1 Cor. 14:34–35).

This means that wives should ask their husbands about doctrine. If husbands do not know or do not want to take the trouble to learn, study, and grow in their thinking as Christians, then they are fools. If a woman is being submissive, it does not follow that she should be ignorant. Women may think they are being traditional by not learning more, but they are actually damaging and destroying future generations. How much your wife knows about the gospel and the doctrines of Christianity is going to be roughly what your sons and daughters know, and also what your grandsons know. Women should know what the gospel is, and they should know the doctrines that are being preached and taught. After all, it is women that are raising up the next generation of preachers. Where did Timothy get his unfeigned faith, if not from his grandmother Lois and mother Eunice (2 Tim. 1:5)?

A PARTNER IN MINISTRY

A godly woman is involved in the mission of the Church. Paul says, "And I intreat thee also, true yokefellow, help those women which laboured with me in the gospel, with Clement also, and with other my fellowlabourers, whose names are in the book of life" (Phil. 4:3). Those who say that evangelism and Bible studies are "just for men" do not get it. Women are not to perform teaching roles over men in the Church, but their ministering role is no less important.

Consider Acts 18:24–26: "And a certain Jew named Apollos, born at Alexandria, an eloquent man, and mighty in the scriptures, came to Ephesus. This man was instructed in the way of the Lord; and being fervent in the spirit, he spake and taught diligently the things of the Lord, knowing only the baptism of John. And he began to speak boldly in the synagogue: whom when Aquila and Priscilla had heard, they took him unto them, and expounded unto him the way of God more perfectly."

We see here that *both* Aquila and Priscilla explain to Apollos that what he was teaching was insufficient. Priscilla here was not teaching in the synagogue, but she was a part of the team out in the parking lot that set Apollos straight. Even though he was an eloquent teacher, mighty in the Scriptures, Priscilla knew more than he did. When it says that women are not to exercise authority over men, this does not mean that men have nothing to learn from women. If my wife tells me about something she noticed in Colossians, it would be stupid for me to try to pretend that "I already knew that."

Women are not just to manage the kitchen and the potluck after church. Christian women are to be as thoughtful and engaged in the work of the Church as the men.

CLOTHING

A godly woman dresses well. Proverbs 31:22 says, "She maketh herself coverings of tapestry; her clothing is silk and purple." Modesty and decorum do not entail dressing in a feed sack.

The Bible does not say that pagan women adorn themselves and Christian women do not. The difference between pagan and Christian women is *how* they adorn themselves, not whether they do. The woman is the crown of her husband, and so she should care how she looks because how she looks reflects on him. If the crown is tarnished, the king looks bad.

When pagan women adorn themselves, they do it out of vain conceit. This is what Peter is talking about when he says, "Whose adorning let it not be that outward adorning of plaiting the hair, and of wearing of gold, or of putting on of apparel; but let it be the hidden man of the heart, in that which is not corruptible, even the ornament of a meek and quiet spirit, which is in the sight of God of great price" (1 Pet. 3:3–4). So the lesson should be that a woman should not be the kind that puts on her makeup with a trowel. She should not put her hair up in ornate braids and then sprinkle gold dust on it, like she was getting ready for a big event at Versailles. Peter is not forbidding pigtails or braids. He is saying that women must not adorn themselves in a way that is outlandish. The godly method of a woman adorning herself results in women who are far more beautiful, far more lovely, far prettier than anything you find out in the world. At the same time, we should not spiritualize this passage. While it is important for women to adorn themselves with a gentle and quiet spirit, women should not think of themselves as above it all when it comes to physical appearances.

Women are the ornament of the Church. In the first few centuries when the gospel was first spreading, the Christian women were well cared for and were especially attractive to the pagan men as a model for what wives should be like. Women should aspire to be like that.

HER HAIR IS GIVEN AS A COVERING

A godly woman honors her husband with her hair for the sake of her husband.

Paul says in 1 Corinthians 11:5–10:

> But every woman that prayeth or prophesieth with her head uncovered dishonoureth her head: for that is even all one as if she were shaven. For if the woman be not covered, let her also be shorn: but if it be a shame for a woman to be shorn or shaven, let her be covered. For a man indeed ought not to cover his head, forasmuch as he is the image and glory of God: but the woman is the glory of the

man. For the man is not of the woman: but the woman of the man. Neither was the man created for the woman; but the woman for the man. For this cause ought the woman to have power on her head because of the angels.

The woman is the man's crown. The crown does not come second: the crown is the capstone, the final glory. When God progresses through His creation week, He progresses from the lesser glory to the greater glory. The first three days of creation are about shaping and dividing, and the second three days are all about adorning. The final act of creation is the creation of the woman, and the woman ought to act as though she is that final glory. Because the woman has that high privilege, a godly woman will know that her hair is a daily sermon on how her husband is doing. Do people look at you and see that you are cared for and that your husband treats you right? Or do they think you are hurting? How a woman presents herself and how she dresses is a statement about the conditions of her home.

A woman who spends more time on her hair than does her husband is not engaging in vanity. Christian women have a high station, and that is why they should care about these things.

CHAPTER 5

The Federal Family

As we have been considering marriage, we have paid close attention to how marriages are covenantal entities. It is the covenant that makes them what they are. Remember, a covenant is not a contract: it is something deeper, thicker, richer than a mere agreement. A covenant is a solemn bond, sovereignly administered, with attendant blessings and curses. Covenants are built into the world, and they cannot be established or disestablished by legislation or social customs. Marriage covenants are rooted in the fact that God has made us male and female, and the two sexes were designed by Him to produce children together. It is not subject to the courts or public opinion.

COVENANT THINKING

As we look into the nature of the covenantal family, consider this passage from the beginning of the book of Job: "And his sons went and feasted in their houses, every one his day; and sent and called for their three sisters to eat and to drink with them. And it was so, when the days of their feasting were gone about, that Job sent and sanctified them, and rose up early in the morning, and offered burnt offerings according to the number of them all: for Job said, It may be that my sons have sinned, and cursed God in their hearts. Thus did Job continually" (1:4–5).

Job does not offer sacrifices because of a feeling of guilt, or to cover for his parental failure; this practice of his is cited as an example of his *righteousness*. Later in the chapter God brags about Job and declares that no one is righteous like him (1:8). This is therefore an example of the kind of thing that a father ought to be doing. Job knew the nature of his responsibility, and he was not the kind of man who made excuses.

This is the opposite of how we usually think about the family. We usually think of the family as a mere social arrangement. But home is more than where you hang your hat. We live in a time when the state is trying to amass as much authority as possible, and so consequently any authority that might be able to stand up to it is challenged. Edmund Burke called these subordinate

authorities "little platoons," because they are entities that
are resistant to the encroachments of the state. If individuals are of primary social importance instead of families,
then we become detached from each other—the state
wants an atomistic society so that we can be easier to
manage or manipulate. However, if these atoms join
together in molecules as families, or complex molecules
like neighborhoods, townships, and congregations, then
they become formidable in the eyes of the state. Their
bonds to each other are stronger than their bonds to a
government agency that is thousands of miles away.

Even if an individual is not married, this does not
mean that he is not part of the program. Everyone is
a brother, a sister, a son, or a daughter in the body of
Christ. We have all sorts of molecular connections,
while marriage is at the center because that is where
we all come from. Enemies can attack it from outside
and idiots can attack it from within, and so it is here
that we have to be particularly careful.

When things are going wrong within the family,
one problem that often appears is that the father tries
to fix the problem by issuing commands. Blockhead
fathers will point to Ephesians 5 and then act surprised
when just telling everybody to submit does not fix all
the problems. That kind of spirit is totally antithetical
to how God established His family. At the same time,
look at Job: he does not go to the Lord in sacrifice and

point to his own godliness and complain about his children's sins. Job takes responsibility—and authority flows to those who take responsibility.

Is your marriage a mess, husbands? Take responsibility, and do not go to your wife just to point out her problems. Do not talk to anybody about the problems within your family except God, and go to Him, taking responsibility for absolutely everything. If you pray like that for a few days, I would be surprised if things do not start to change with your wife and children. That kind of spirit and attitude is transformational.

Brittle, ego-driven masculinity wants to blame other people for the problems. "If you would only" . . . "I can't believe you didn't . . ." This blame-shifting is the antithesis of masculinity. Taking responsibility means going to God and admitting that He has a problem with your family and that as the head you are the one who is responsible. Ask God to deal with *you*. And do not try to manipulate your wife by telling her that you will take responsibility for all the things that she is doing wrong. This business must be transacted between you and God alone, and nobody else should know a thing about it. If you do this, then you will find that authority will start to flow to you, precisely because you have gladly accepted responsibility.

Jesus once said this: "The kings of the Gentiles exercise lordship over them; and they that exercise authority upon them are called benefactors. But ye shall not be so: but he that is greatest among you, let him be as the younger; and he that is chief, as he that doth serve" (Luke 22:25–26). The Bible is a patriarchal book in which fathers are the head of the household, but Jesus says here that we are not supposed to have an authority that is domineering. A man does not achieve authority by yelling or quoting Bible verses. He gets authority by being like Jesus, who got on His hands and knees and washed the disciples' feet: "So after he had washed their feet, and had taken his garments, and was set down again, he said unto them, Know ye what I have done to you? Ye call me Master and Lord: and ye say well; for so I am. If I then, your Lord and Master, have washed your feet; ye also ought to wash one another's feet. For I have given you an example, that ye should do as I have done to you. Verily, verily, I say unto you, The servant is not greater than his lord; neither he that is sent greater than he that sent him" (John 13:12–16).

This is particularly the case for parents. Parents frequently struggle with the issues surrounding personal responsibility because our age has taught them to think so individualistically. Now, children are responsible for their own behavior and need to be taught how to confess their own sins, but as we see with Job, parents should *also* take responsibility for things that their children have done. This does not absolve their children of their

personal responsibility; rather, the person under authority is learning by example how to live responsibly. He
will grow up to be the kind of adult who takes responsibility for himself because of what he saw growing up.

If a son is not taking responsibility for his actions,
chances are good he learned that evasiveness from his
father. But if the father takes responsibility for his son,
then he is far more likely to bring his son to real repen-
tance when he tries to get his son to take responsibility
for his actions. We think that responsibility is something that is split between people, but in the world of
covenants, responsibility is not something that can be
divided up 50/50, or even 70/30—taking responsibility is not a zero-sum game. It is something that mul-
tiplies and increases as one party takes responsibility.
If a father takes responsibility for how his son is doing
spiritually, that does not leave less responsibility for his
son to take. It leaves more.

Jesus died for our sins. Does that make us feel more
or less responsible for how we live? We should feel less
guilty and less condemned because we have been liberated and forgiven. At the same time, we know we
are not supposed to go live like the devil just because
we have been saved. As Paul put it, "What shall we say
then? Shall we continue in sin, that grace may abound?
God forbid. How shall we, that are dead to sin, live
any longer therein?" (Rom. 6:1–2). When Jesus took

responsibility for us on the cross, that liberated us. Husbands and fathers are not told to duplicate what Jesus did, but they are told to imitate it. And so federal responsibility does not diminish other people's responsibility but rather increases it.

This way of thinking enables us to think of the family as a united entity. The covenant family is a real thing that God sees and interacts with; a man has individual responsibilities, but he also has corporate responsibilities that are every bit as real. We live in an individualistic age where everything outside our own ego space is considered arbitrary. We do not want to abandon that only to adopt a hive mentality—in such a case, we would just be veering from a ditch on one side of the road to the ditch on the other. But biblical living means acknowledging the corporate entities we are a part of, such as the family and the Church, and that will in turn heighten our individual responsibilities as Christians.

Wives who are submissive are not swallowed up into their husband's identity, and husbands who take responsibility for their families do not have their personalities annihilated either. They grow into real, three-dimensional characters. This is something that is hard to do but not that difficult to understand. Swallow your pride, and do what you need to do. If you are a father or a husband, go out into the backyard, look at the stars, and take responsibility before God for *everything* in your house—this is not just hard but impossible. So go to God and admit that it is all your responsibility, that much of it is your fault, and that you have nothing to plead except the blood of Jesus Christ. Then ask Him to help you take responsibility.

This is hard to do because you were not the one who ran up the charges on the credit card, you did not talk back, you did not stay out past curfew. You did all the "right things," and you feel you are the only one doing *anything* right. You do not want to be blamed for things you did not do. However, you are content with Jesus taking responsibility for things *He* did not do. Remember, this is the absolute center of the Christian faith.

The most important thing that ever happened on the planet was the Messiah taking responsibility for things He did not do, and learning to imitate this is the game plan for how we are going to conquer the world. We think that it's "not fair" that we have to take responsibility for things that are not our fault—even though our salvation was not fair at all. We are like the unforgiving servant in the parable who was forgiven a debt of $10 million and then went out and found somebody else who owed him a quarter and started to choke him for it. What we need to understand is that this is God's strategy for liberation.

When a man drives straight into a brick wall at this point, he should find that the brick wall is made out of his pride. Only God can deal with such pride, and so he needs to ask God to take down any barrier that he has built up inside himself that insists on not being held responsible for the things that others in his family did. Take out this trash, and when you go back in and have a conversation with your wife, she will wonder what happened to you. Humble yourself under the mighty hand of God, and He will lift you up (1 Pet. 5:6).

Apart from this kind of thinking, an adversarial spirit will develop within the family: "You are over there, and I am over here, and we each have our own perspective." Covenantal thinking is the basis for even being able to *say* "we." When a man takes responsibility for the things the kids might be thinking in their hearts, he does this in the name of Jesus. When he prays, he concludes that prayer with "in Jesus's name, Amen." This is the fulfillment of all the animal sacrifices found in Leviticus. When Israelites prayed in the Old Testament, they prayed that God would bless their households in the coming year. We should pray the same, but we do so in the name of the Messiah, who has already come and fulfilled all the promises.

Every doctrine lives as it is applied through obedience, and not by being applied as a technique or life hack. Americans love techniques where there are several steps to do this or that, or some secret formula that would work no matter where the heart is. But this is not technique—it is a mind of wisdom. Wisdom cannot be plugged in to run automatically, regardless of where the mind and heart are. We all have to respond to the call of God and the authority of His Word.

COVENANTAL UNITY

When the covenantal head makes a decision, the family makes a decision—the fact that it was the head who made the decision does not change that the decision was made, and made on behalf of all. If my head decides to go somewhere, my feet take me there. But if the head says north and the body says south, there is a problem. The head cannot *solve* the problem by turning and yelling at the body. The head must not ask the body what the problem is; instead, it must ask God how it can take responsibility for the body as a more effective head.

The reluctance that many heads have when it comes to taking responsibility is the reason the head and body go in opposite directions. So the head should ask God what He wants the head to learn. The best place to put this into practice is in the husband's prayer life—this should not creep into his conversations, because our hearts are deceitfully wicked and it is easy to use this kind of thing in a manipulative way. If it is just the husband and his God, the only place it will "come out" is when he is taking responsibility. We believe that God is the living God, and so when we talk to Him, we are doing business on a more profound level than anything we do anywhere else in our lives. We feel often when we pray that we are just talking to the ceiling and that we are not accomplishing anything. Usually this is a consequence of how we pray—we pray: "God, please bless America generally speaking," or "God, please do any number of nondescript generic things so that no one will ever be able to tell whether or not you have answered the request." There is really no way to tell whether a vague prayer has been answered or not.

There are two types of prayers that we are reluctant to offer up to God. We are reluctant to pray prayers that we know are *not* in the will of God. If we asked God for three red Lamborghinis, and a garage to put them in, or ten freezers filled with cookie dough ice cream, this would be a very specific prayer, but it still is a bad prayer. As James says, "Ye lust, and have not: ye kill, and desire to have, and cannot obtain: ye fight and war, yet ye have not, because ye ask not. Ye ask, and receive not, because ye ask amiss, that ye may consume it upon your lusts" (Jas. 4:2–3).

So we know that it is bad to pray self-centered prayers. We do not pray for three red Lamborghinis, because we are rightly afraid God will say no. But there is another type of prayer we avoid because we are afraid

God will say *yes*: "Lord, I know that I am not a patient man, and so I am asking that you would give me a series of trials this week so I could grow in patience." The reason that kind of prayer sticks in our craw is because we know what God is like—if we prayed like that, He would send us trials, and then we would have to learn patience, just like we requested. When we are struggling to pray this way, it is *not* because we are afraid we are talking to the ceiling. It might be the first prayer in months or years where the request was for God to mess up your life, and you are pretty confident He will.

So, ask God to unsettle everything. Ask God to enter your marriage and family and to knock down all the brittle faux masculinity in order to shatter it. God will not despise such a prayer. If a man says, "Lord, mess up this family," He will do it and there will no longer be a complacent, disobedient marriage anymore. Many of us do not want radical Christianity, radical discipleship, or radical responsibility to come in and disrupt everything.

If a father catches his son watching porn, should he say, "That's not how we taught him. He should know better. I can't believe after all we taught him and after all the times we took him to church, he would go and do this." That is anti-covenantal thinking. Covenantal thinking works this way: "Father in Heaven, it looks as though lust has taken a foothold in our house. We come before you in the name of Jesus to confess our responsibility for what has happened here." When a man thinks in terms of covenantal solidarity, he is teaching his kids to do the same, instead of teaching *them* to blame others and make excuses.

Taking another example, suppose the father is deciding which restaurant to go to in a big city, and the wife and kids are all chiming in with their various preferences. There are many different ideas, but someone needs to make a decision. If it were up for a vote, there would be a tie and so someone has to decide. Suppose the father goes to the restaurant his wife wants to go to, and suppose it is closed, and they find out the other restaurant contender is running a big special, and it is too far to go there now. If the husband wheels on the wife and blames her for the decision, that is anti-covenantal thinking. It is a petty decision, but it still reveals anti-covenantal thinking. *He* made the decision. If his wife feels bad about it, he should say, "Oh, no, this is fine. That's just the way it goes. I made the decision." This may be a trivial example, but for so many men this is the entire battle.

This way of thinking does not come naturally, but it provides a powerful example. If the kids start squabbling in the back about it, then Dad can speak to that situation and tell the kids not to blame each other. And he has the moral authority now to do that. It may seem like a light and trivial thing, but it is the pattern that God has set before us.

CHAPTER 6

Common Sins of the Household

In a chapter like this, there are some obvious sins that it would be easy to focus on (e.g., complaining, fighting, disobeying, etc.), since those are sins that are obvious and disruptive. However, we sometimes need to take a step or two back and address problems that set us up for temptation, rather than focusing on the immediate sins themselves. Obvious and glaring sins are not as dangerous as the sins that we believe to be virtues. This is why, for example, Jesus said that prostitutes and tax collectors were closer to the kingdom of Heaven than the well-respected theologians of His day—the tax collectors and sinners *knew* they had a problem, but the self-righteous Pharisees did not know that sin had them by the throat. They thought they were virtuous and wise when they were really white-washed tombs.

The word *Pharisee* used to be a term of high respect. The closest modern equivalent would be the term *Puritan*. The root of the word *Pharisee* means "to separate," and the Pharisees were a movement that tried to separate themselves from ungodliness so they could be holy; they took rules that applied to the priesthood and sought to apply them to the whole nation of Israel, and they were highly respected in their day. Then Jesus came and trashed their name forever, simply by teaching the world that their virtues were actually vices. This is why we should know that we often have to repent of our virtues as much as our vices.

THE CONCERN

Malachi says this towards the end of his book: "Behold, I will send you Elijah the prophet before the coming of the great and dreadful day of the Lord: And he shall turn the heart of the fathers to the children, and the heart of the children to their fathers, lest I come and smite the earth with a curse" (Mal. 4:5–6). This is a prophecy about John the Baptist, and it shows that he was meant to turn the hearts of fathers and children towards each other. When fathers and mothers are honored, the result is blessing in the land; when things are bad in the home, God strikes the land with a curse. This means we cannot look at the condition of our country today and not bring an indictment on the American home.

In Ephesians, Paul quotes the Ten Commandments and makes this point: "Children, obey your parents in the Lord: for this is right. Honour thy father and mother; which is the first commandment with a promise; that it may be well with thee, and thou mayest live long on the earth. And, ye fathers, provoke not your children to wrath: but bring them up in the nurture and admonition of the Lord" (6:1–4). Paul takes an old covenant promise and applies it to a new covenant Gentile Church—there is still a blessing for obedience and also a warning for disobedience. When fathers and mothers are harsh in the name of righteousness, the results are devastating; when the family breaks down, everything breaks down. You cannot really have a stable country, nation, or tribe, if all the families are disintegrating.

It is no coincidence that we are fighting a battle over the definition of marriage. If we allow for no-fault divorce, then it will not be long before we lose the proper definition of the family. As this has happened, some people have reacted and pulled away from the modern world—people retreat to gingham dresses and prairie-muffin aesthetics. However, having "traditional family values" does not prevent families from breaking down, and indeed many of the greatest moral failures have manifested themselves in the traditionalist camp. If we all retreat into our traditionalist enclaves, then all the same corruptions will erupt inside them.

Where does all this come from? Paul gives us the answer: "Wherefore if ye be dead with Christ from the rudiments of the world, why, as though living in the world, are ye subject to ordinances, (Touch not; taste not; handle not; which all are to perish with the using;) after the commandments and doctrines of men? Which things have indeed a shew of wisdom in will worship, and humility, and neglecting of the body: not in any honour to the satisfying of the flesh" (Col. 2:20–23). We might add, "dance not," "drink not," "smoke not." Paul says these things have an appearance of wisdom but are of *no use* in subduing the flesh. Another translation describes it as having no value in "checking self-indulgence" (NRSV).

Strict rules do not fix the problem. Retreating into an enclave does not fix the problem. Building a neo-Amish compound does not fix the problem. The old Adam will follow you in there. Because wherever a man goes, there he is. If a bunch of sinners try to retreat into the woods and build a society there, it turns out that this new society is also made up of sinners. Unless there is something that addresses *that*, the proffered fix is not going to solve anything. The thing that does address it is the grace of God in Jesus Christ. It is the gospel, not the law, that enables us to live in accordance with God's standards.

In the cultural battles that we are in, many traditionalist parents have sought to fight the corruption of the age by retreating and building walls made out of laws and rules. If you homeschool or build a Christian school and then man it with a high-tech security system that is guaranteed to keep sin out, then *nobody* is going to be able to get in. So we need something that really deals with sin. We want to have congregations that want to live in accordance with the Word of God and have high standards, and all of it *grounded in grace*. The temptation will be to have the wrong kind of high standards, and so we must think biblically about issues like schooling, because there is no formula for schooling or family culture that you can just plug in and have everything turn out great automatically. We are to live by faith in Christ, not by faith in our rules.

If we look at the children after church running around, we need to realize that there is an entire minicongregation down there being shaped, exhorted, rebuked, and taught about how to approach God and His world. If they are not being taught in accordance with the grace of God, then it will all come crashing down. The old joke is that you can always tell a Harvard man, but you can't tell him much. In the same way, we can always tell a person who has his educational theories lined up about how he is going to do it. Someone else might have a really good observation about the plan, but he will not listen, because his theories get in the way.

If you have ever worked construction, you know that once you pour the concrete foundation of a house, a couple hours later you are all done. If a hard-headed father is in the grip of a bunch of delusional thoughts about how to raise children, by the time he realizes what things are *actually* like, the concrete has already hardened. You have a situation on your hands, and although there is still hope for God's intervention, the ordinary time within which parents may raise their children to love the ways of God has passed. If a couple have knee-high children, they should want to be solidly based in Scripture while there is still time. Nobody wants to have regrets fifteen years down the road after having ignored this advice. If we are carefully observing other people's kids, we can often see a car wreck coming years down the road, even though the people currently behind the wheel cannot see it.

I am very grateful that many parents are committed to Christian education, but this is not an automatic solution. We can have disasters come out of strict homeschools. We can have terrible disasters in classical Christian schools. Many schools think that classical education should be hard, and since eating gravel is hard, they make all the kids eat gravel and call it classical education. A lot of spiritual energy could be spared if we consider some of the root problems.

YOU CAN'T GIVE WHAT YOU DON'T HAVE

In the parable of the sower, Jesus described the seed that fell among thorns: "And that which fell among thorns are they, which, when they have heard, go forth, and are choked with cares and riches and pleasures of this life, and bring no fruit to perfection" (Luke 8:14). Now this passage is addressing people concerned with the pleasures of this life and with riches, but it also applies more broadly to those who are concerned with the cares of this life, and ordinary family life is often crammed full of those. Those who do not know the nature of their own souls are in no position to shepherd others. Those who do not know how it is between them and God are in no position to determine how things are between God and their children.

So parents should take care not to neglect the state of their own souls. Busyness is not holiness, and it is often at war with it. You can be shuttling people to and from godly opportunities and yet be neglecting your own time in the Word, not to mention your prayers. If father and mother just spend all day pouring themselves out for the kids, and then collapse at the end of the day, it is not good if you have not reserved enough time to consider your own soul. If a parent is starving, he will not be able to feed anyone else. Parental famine won't fill the cupboards of the children. Even if they have a good school or good curriculum, the children will not be fed by God in the same way unless they have good and godly parents who are good and godly Christians.

I do not want to imply that if parents are languishing there is nothing God can do. Many Christians grew up in non-Christian homes and God still intervened in their lives, and God can do the same for wayward children as well. But this is like asking whether we can glorify God in a plane crash. That does happen, and people do walk away from plane crashes, but we do not plan for that kind of thing: in the ordinary course of events, we want a smooth plane ride.

NO FAMILY IS AN ISLAND

Parents must be careful not to adopt a defensive isolationism. When Paul addresses families, he does so within the context of instructions to the whole Church. In places such as Ephesians 5–6 and Colossians 3, Paul addresses wives, husbands, children, and fathers, and he is doing so all together. The commands to particular family members are written in a letter to a church.

Christians are to live in community, and this means that we are involved in one another's lives and with one another's children. When we conduct baptisms at our church, we take vows as a congregation to help the parents raise these children in the fear and admonition of the Lord. This does not mean we are to step into the role of a self-appointed helper, but we are also not to be disengaged or detached. Some people are closer than others—some people are family members and others are just acquaintances—but nobody can say he has nothing to do with those kids running around over there. Covenants do not just hold the family together: they also hold families together.

Many parents falsely assume they know their children better than anyone else in the Church does. But it would be more accurate to say that parents *could* know their children better if they studied the Word and their children with biblical wisdom. If they did, then they would know that the wounds of a friend are faithful, while the kisses of an enemy are deceitful (Prov. 27:6). There are ways parents naturally know their children better than anyone else, and there are ways complete strangers know what your kid is up to way better than you do. This is because Mom justifies everything and thinks that a "good talk" can fix it, while often the stranger on the bus can see that Mom is getting played like a violin. While Mom knows the child's middle name, and the observer at church does not, the observer at church might know that the child is full of deep cunning that has his mother snowed.

It is hard for us when someone comes up and says something our kid did was wrong, sinful, or shameful. Of course, there are times when parents should stand up for their child, but your operating assumption should *not* be to side with your child against anybody else automatically. If parents *automatically* side with their own children, they are going to be wrong more often than they are going to be right. We are not born with eyes in the back of our heads.

At the same time, the neighbors do not have most of the backstory to your kids and they do not know all the challenges. So when we offer counsel to someone, it should be with fear and trembling, and we should not set ourselves up to personally rebuke all the parents in the church. But if you see something, and the parents are missing it, then you should go with an inquiry for them.

Paul discusses the spirit in which we are to do this: "Brethren, if a man be overtaken in a fault, ye which are spiritual, restore such an one in the spirit of meekness; considering thyself, lest thou also be tempted" (Gal. 6:1). When someone sees a problem on the playground that the parents are not aware of, that someone needs to tell them about it. At the same time, this should not be done in a spirit of accusation. Instead, the approach should be something like, "Are you open to me sharing some things that I thought you might want to know?" Do not accuse. Do not point the finger. But neither should a concerned brother keep his mouth closed.

The brother may feel he does not want to start fights with families all over the church, but the alternative sometimes is waiting until these stinkers grow up and fight with each other. Sin never gets better when we wink at it. There are many situations where someone must screw up his courage and talk to his friends about how their kids are out of control. It is not necessary to use the words *hellions*, *banshees*, or *rapscallions*. The point can be made more delicately. He might not feel confident, especially if last week it was his own kid that was out of control, but the issue should not be whether any given child was a sinner—the issue should be whether it was dealt with. All kids need their diapers changed, and the good parent is the one who cleans it up, not the one who never has to change the dirty diapers. Are the parents dealing with the problem? Are they engaged with their children? When a child flops on the floor or has an outburst of rage, does Dad take the kid away and deal with the problem? Nobody should have an issue when the parents are dealing with the problem.

We have all been there. The only problem that arises is when the parents seem to be oblivious to the problem, or they recognize it but layer over it with excuses. "He didn't have his nap today . . ."

We all want to live in community, and that means saying something when it is appropriate, and keeping our mouth shut when *that* is appropriate. We should all be praying actively to learn the difference.

IGNORANT ISOLATION

Sin seeks out darkness: "And this is the condemnation, that light is come into the world, and men loved darkness rather than light, because their deeds were evil" (John 3:19). Paul also warns us about this: "For we dare not make ourselves of the number, or compare ourselves with some that commend themselves: but they measuring themselves by themselves, and comparing themselves among themselves, are not wise" (2 Cor. 10:12).

Notice that the sin here is comparing oneself only to those within a small, selected set. This sadly is a common problem among those who homeschool. If a parent is trying to gauge where the children are, it is necessary to have external benchmarks. If those are missing, often, when problems arise, they are not identified until it is too late.

Imagine four lanes, two going one way and two going the other—two lanes going to Heaven and two going to Hell. On the road to Heaven there is a Ford and a Chevy, and on the road to Hell there is a Ford and a Chevy. Often when the Chevys pass each other, the owners wave and beep at each other because of all they share in common. But while they may share the same make of car, they are going in *opposite directions*. The issue is not homeschooling or classroom schooling. You have wise and foolish people using both methods. Godly homeschooling parents and godly parents who have their children enrolled in a good school are using different methods to drive in the same direction.

I have written elsewhere on the importance of maintaining the distinction between principles and methods. Families do things differently, but if they are pursuing the same biblical principles, it is foolish to bother them just because they do not share the same method. This does not mean that what the children in another household are doing is none of our concern: we are in community with one another, and we should note our various strengths and weaknesses. Many times, homeschoolers neglect academics because the parents say that they want to emphasize character over studies, and so they let the kids run around in the meadow. However, such parents are actually *neglecting* character, because academic work *is* a character issue.

Parents need to make sure they are looking around and getting outside counsel as needed. The besetting sin of homeschoolers is the sin of tuning out criticism—when criticism comes, you get defensive, and you get your back up. So if parents are homeschooling and someone rebukes them, the godly response is to consider it oil on the head, *even if the correction is in error.* The best thing is to listen to the criticism and bring it before God. Nobody wants to be blown back and forth by whatever people say, but everyone should want to be open to learn. So those parents who are homeschooling, where this applies, lose the defensiveness.

PART OF THE CROWD

The next common sin is more prevalent among those parents who use a Christian school with traditional classrooms. Far from neglecting community, presumption is a sin that relies entirely upon community. All the parents need to do is enroll the children in the Christian school, attend church, and hang around fellow Christians, and everything will magically turn out alright. But when parents do not exercise godly and wise and ongoing oversight over their children, bad things will happen regardless of the community in which they live. A person can flunk out of the best school in the world. Those who educate their children this way are tempted to put their kids into a godly cluster, and because all the other godly people are standing upright, they think it will keep their kid propped up. This is not bringing up your children in the nurture and admonition of the Lord.

Nancy and I sent our kids to a classical Christian school, but we spent countless hours at the dinner table debriefing from the day. We would tell our kids, "If someone says this to you on the playground, this is how you should react." The next day it would be something else. We were actively engaged with whatever was happening. But there are unfortunately many parents who just drop their kids off at the school with the tuition check and then check out. And sometimes they forget the tuition check. But all parents need to have friends and family who are willing to bring a friend up short and point out when a child is not thriving in a class, or when he is not standing up to the worldliness that can be manifested in every school.

Paul says, "That we henceforth be no more children, tossed to and fro, and carried about with every wind of doctrine, by the sleight of men, and cunning craftiness, whereby they lie in wait to deceive" (Eph. 4:14). There are two types of people who fit this description. There are people who do things that are obviously foolish and destructive—this would include loose living, unbiblical standards, and the fads that people chase after—this is obvious, and in the end what we have is a big smoking crater. But then there are people who do all sorts of things that *could* be fruitful and could be constructive if only pursued with wisdom. This is where conservative Christians pursuing a Christian education can falter. The first problem is that of being unbiblical. The second is a problem found in the adverbs—they are being biblical . . . unbiblically.

For example, courtship is something I have written about, and I have seen a lot of people pursue it wisely. But I have also seen a lot of people pursue it very foolishly. Courtship and a Christian education are both good things, and they can be implemented by wise people, but stampedes never bring wisdom. Bad things implemented stupidly do a lot of damage; good things implemented stupidly can do even more. If a man does a stupid thing badly, nobody is surprised. But when he does a good thing stupidly, everybody suddenly wonders what happened.

Reformation is never brought about by plugging in a formula. This includes practical things like education, childrearing, and marriage. These are not things where you can just do the drill without reflection, without wisdom, without obedience, or without love. If you just do the drill, you will create something suffocating. Our task as parents is not to get your kids to conform to the standard: *our job is to get them to love the standard.*

Fathers, your kids will love the standard when you love God and you love their mother. In that context of love and mercy created by the gospel alone, a man should pursue high standards. When a man imitates the wise, he grows. When he just copies the wise, nothing much happens. This is because when a man imitates the wise, he is growing from the inside. If he copies the wise, it is a purely external sort of thing. There are people who want to preach like Billy Graham and so they buy the floppy Bible—but that does not make them able to preach like Billy Graham. It is all foam, no beer, so to speak. All floppy Bible, no unction.

Imitation is based on the cross. Look at Jesus Christ dying, buried, resurrected. Imitate Him, and imitate those who are imitating Him. This is what will make us able to be transformed from the inside out. Jesus said that if we wash the inside of the cup, the outside will be clean (Matt. 23:26). If we are just copying, then we are rinsing just the outside of the cup. If we simply copy, we are just leaving room for lots of sin inside, and no matter what method we are using, it will never work.

But if we imitate and love Jesus together, the family will laugh together, play together, pray together, and go to church together. And go to Heaven together. It will be good.

CHAPTER 7

Sketch of Godly Parents

The heart of all parenting is faith. If we are Christians, we live and we die by faith. One of the great recoveries of the Reformation was the doctrine of *sola fide*—justification by faith alone—and it is faith that governs everything we do. This is not just for justification, but sanctification is also by faith. As Paul says, "For I am not ashamed of the gospel of Christ: for it is the power of God unto salvation to every one that believeth; to the Jew first, and also to the Greek. For therein is the righteousness of God revealed from faith to faith: as it is written, The just shall live by faith" (Rom. 1:16–17).

Paul does not just say that the just *start* by faith: he says the just will *live* by faith. The parental task of bringing up children in the fear and admonition of the Lord should be governed by faith. The vows and promises that parents make to raise their kids when they have them baptized are vows that cannot be kept by works, by striving, or by trying harder. They have to be kept by receiving God's gracious gospel promise in faith. This is the only way.

KEEPING COVENANT

"Know therefore that the Lord thy God, he is God, the faithful God, which keepeth covenant and mercy with them that love him and keep his commandments to a thousand generations" (Deut. 7:9).

Here we see that God keeps covenant for a thousand generations. This is particularly interesting because the human race has not even had a thousand generations yet. God's covenant grace extends to generation after generation, and it is our blessed task to receive this stupefying promise by faith.

"Then said they unto him, What shall we do, that we might work the works of God? Jesus answered and said unto them, This is the work of God, that ye believe on him whom he hath sent" (John 6:28–29).

Jesus does not tell them that our work is to strive harder, or to pick up big heavy weights and carry them to Heaven. He tells His disciples to believe in Him. He wants us to believe what God declares in His gospel, and so our task is to respond with faith. God is the one who keeps us secure, and so when we are wondering what we are to do as a parent, we should be characterized by faith. Godly parents should therefore be confident, trusting, quiet, and serene.

Now of course, godly parenting means exhibiting good works. The next-door neighbors should see you *doing* a lot of stuff. They do not see you lounging on the sofa inside, trusting God, as your kids run around feral and wild. We do not just wait for God's lightning bolt of grace to strike the kids because . . . *soli Deo gloria*. People looking on from the side will see godly parents doing a lot, but we are Christians saved by grace, not by good works. At the same time, while we are not saved *by* good works, we are saved *to* good works, which is what the neighbors see: "For by grace are ye saved through faith; and that not of yourselves: it is the gift of God: Not of works, lest any man should boast. For we are his workmanship, created in Christ Jesus unto good works, which God hath before ordained that we should walk in them" (Eph. 4:8–10). God wants us to be doing good works, and when we do them, they are visible to other people. These other people think that what they see us doing is the secret, but these works are simply the overflow of faith. We do not trust in our

works, but we overflow with them because of the confidence we have in God. The works of godly parents
will exceed the righteousness of the Pharisees, but they
will not dream of trusting in them.

Paul says, "Wherefore, my beloved, as ye have always
obeyed, not as in my presence only, but now much
more in my absence, work out your own salvation with
fear and trembling. For it is God which worketh in
you both to will and to do of his good pleasure" (Phil.
2:12–13). We are to work out what God works in.
God accomplishes our salvation outside of us and then
declares what He has done to us. We respond in faith,
which is God taking His work and working it into us.
Then, as a result of God working in us, we work it out.
Therefore parents are to give to their kids what God
gave in order to give to them. Parents are not to give
their kids things that *they* cooked up or invented.

No one can be justified or sanctified by their works,
and therefore parents cannot sanctify their kids by
works. If parents get up in front of a church, make
promises, and then invite the pastor to get the kid wet,
and this is done on the basis of their own name and
authority, it is the sin of being presumptuous. We cannot do any of this by our own authority. One time,
Charles Spurgeon was talking to a man, and the man
said, "When I got saved, God did His part, and I did
mine." Spurgeon's internal alarm bells went off, and

he asked the man what he meant. The man answered, quite correctly, "God saved me, and I got in the way."

The only thing the sinner brings is the sin that needs to be forgiven. We can only be faithful to the covenant by faithfully responding to this truth, and just admitting that God does it all. We know all sorts of ways to get this wrong. For example, we will say we are justified by knowing that God alone justifies us. But God's grace humbles the proud, and this is why we want to turn anything into a work. We want to grab everything and make it ours, but it is all of Christ.

We see in Scripture that there are two basic categories of people: covenant-breakers and covenant-keepers. We all tend to assume that covenant-keeping is done on the basis of works, but covenants with God are always kept by faith alone, and faith only comes through hearing the Word of God. We respond to the declaration of the Word of God. Christ is set before us as crucified, and we hear it. Trusting in our works is how we *break* the covenant. God has made promises to our children, and you do not appropriate that promise through what you do.

COVENANT BLESSINGS

Who is God promising blessings to? Notice what Peter says at the end of Pentecost: "Now when they heard this, they were pricked in their heart, and said unto Peter and to the rest of the apostles, Men and brethren, what shall we do? Then Peter said unto them, Repent, and be baptized every one of you in the name of Jesus Christ for the remission of sins, and ye shall receive the gift of the Holy Ghost. For the promise is unto you, and to your children, and to all that are afar off, even as many as the Lord our God shall call" (Acts 2:37–39).

Notice that the promise offered *to their children* is the promise of the Holy Spirit. How is this possible? "And the Redeemer shall come to Zion, and unto them that turn from transgression in Jacob, saith the Lord. As for me, *this is my covenant* with them, saith the Lord; My spirit that is upon thee, and my words which I have put in thy mouth, shall not depart out of thy mouth, nor out of the mouth of thy seed, nor out of the mouth of thy seed's seed, saith the Lord, from henceforth and for ever" (Isa. 59:20–21, emphasis added). What is the promise that the Lord commits Himself to? It is the promise that He will put the Spirit in Isaiah's mouth and in the mouth of his descendants. This promise is what Peter knew about when he preached his sermon at Pentecost. They knew there would come a day when the great things they heard read in the synagogues would be fulfilled, and that God would keep His promises to a thousand generations, to those who keep covenant.

Now, not everyone who is in the covenant keeps covenant with God. Not everyone who places their children in the covenant by baptism keeps the covenant. So when parents undertake the solemn responsibility of vowing before God and witnesses that they are going to bring up a child in the nurture and admonition of the Lord, this should be a glad, joyful, and terrifying experience. There are only two possible destinations for human beings, and the child that God has entrusted to you is going to live with God forever, or not.

God offers to give us our children and grandchildren and great-grandchildren. We did not earn our children, and so we should receive them as a blessing, *freely given*. Simply being in the covenant is insufficient—we cannot just say that we are Christians, and then just let the kids do whatever they want, making their own decisions. God keeps His promises to those who *keep* covenant, not just to those who are *in* the covenant.

So what do we do to keep covenant? There is a kind of frenetic childrearing where the parents try to oversee and monitor absolutely everything that the child does, because they do not want *anything* to go wrong. This is a problem because they are trying to manage and control this process so that they can wrangle the kids a seat on the bus to Heaven. But the only way to keep the covenant is by faith in God, and not by works. The reason many parents are so anxious and worried about their children is because they are still trusting in their works. Some parents look at their works and *know* they are insufficient, and that is the path to despair. They give up, spin the wheel, and hope for the best—all they can do for their children is pray for them . . . and worry.

On the opposite end of the spectrum, other parents look at their own works and they are confident for some reason. They have taken the seminars and read the books. They have devotional time at the dinner table, and they take the kids to church, to youth group, to Sunday School. These parents are filled with presumption because they are trusting in their works and not in the work of God. It is astounding how many parents can go this route and still lose their kids—and so few notice. For us, the issue boils down to the fact that there is no hope in man. Our only hope is in the promise of God, who has brought us into His household.

Here is a slightly exaggerated illustration: imagine a kid comes from the backyard and asks, "Why are we Christians?" The dad looks up from the sofa and explains that their family follows Jesus Christ and then lays out the gospel. Suppose the kid says he does not want to do all this, only to hear Dad say, "Too bad, we're in this together. You're still going to Heaven. And that means you are going to be holy also. Like it or not." It may seem crazy to have this kind of quiet confidence, but it is our duty simply to believe: this is just the way it is. This is not presumption, though some might call it that.

I grew up in a godly home, and all my life I could no more imagine not being a Christian than I could imagine flying to the moon or living under the ocean. I could not even get my head around it. Why is that? My dad and mom believed the promises.

CONSTANT FAITH

Real faith is constant. The belief we exhibit toward God is not a sporadic or momentary thing. We do not want to parent our children in fits and starts. We are Christians: we follow Jesus, and this is the way it is. We are going to live that around the dinner table, when we rise up and walk along the road, and when we sit down together as a family. Everything should be done in the presence of God.

In the ministry of the Word, we hear God's promises and believe. Assurance and presumption might look very similar from a distance, but the people who know you and know how your family actually operates will be able to tell the difference. They will recognize the *joy* that is characteristic of the family. Presumption comes from the merit of man. Assurance comes from the merit of Jesus Christ, and it trusts in the gracious promises of God.

Many of the people reading this book are probably ancestors of hundreds of thousands of people.

Centuries from now, there will be people on this planet who would not be on this planet had they not met their wives and had children. God has promised them. We cannot see our great-great-grandchildren, but we can trust God for them, and we can love our children for their sake. So love your children. Love your grand-children. Embrace them all, trust God for them, and receive His promises for them.

THE ORDINARY COURSE OF EVENTS

Time and history matter in our lives. We cannot believe in God's promises for the salvation of a child if that child has already died in rebellion. There is a time of oppor-tunity, and there is a time when it is too late. Now, if a child has grown up and is in rebellion, God can still show grace and mercy, but this mercy would not be an ordinary fulfillment of a covenant promise. To covenant parents, there is an ordinary course of events in which a child is given to them, they dedicate the child to God, they make covenant promises in God's presence, and they endeavor to live by God's grace. This is how God loves to bless His children in the ordinary way of the covenant.

God also loves to intervene and save people. Paul was a covenant child who went far astray. He was perse-cuting the Church, breathing out threats and murder against Christians, and God saved him and used him to write the majority of the New Testament. God does it both ways. He brings up faithful covenant children, and He also provides us with remarkable testimonies. At the same time, it is the parents' duty to give their children a boring testimony. Nobody wants their child to be pardoned by the governor while he is on death row for the triple murder of fellow drug lords. That might make for a great testimony at a Sunday evening service somewhere, but it is not what we *want*. I grew up in a tradition where that kind of remarkable testimony was the gold standard. The church would bring in a speaker who had a terrible, scrambled life, and then the kids would groan that they could never be like that. In such cases, Mom should glare down the pew at them, as much as to say that they *better not* be like that.

God wants normal people to bring up children who love their God because they are following their parents' lead. There is nothing disgraceful about that. If the parents have loved their children with gospel truth and they come to love the God who made it possible for them to love in that way, there is nothing wrong with it. This is what we are called to. This is normal.

SOVEREIGNTY AND ELECTION

When parents panic, one of the questions they might ask is whether their children are elect. Whenever this question comes up, we need to distinguish between doubts and questions. Questions have answers; doubts never do. Doubts begin with "What if . . .?" If a person has a question, he can research it, study the Word of God, and then come up with an answer. But he cannot successfully answer a doubt.

Suppose a wife is doing the dishes and the thought comes to her head unbidden that her husband might not be faithful. Let us say she has no grounds for suspicion at all. What is the reason for such a doubt? The only way to answer that kind of doubt is to say, "Well, what if he is faithful?" She has no evidence and nothing to go on. She must laugh at doubt, not giving it the time of day.

However, if the wife doing the dishes sees a blonde in a red convertible out in front of the house, honking for her husband, and she wonders then if her husband is faithful, that is a reasonable *question*. That is a question, not a doubt, and this is because questions have answers in principle. And, in this case, it had better be a good one. If a Christian is wondering why the Bible says something here and something else over there, and wonders how to reconcile them, that is something he can study to find the answer. It is a question. Why does Paul say we are justified apart from the works of the law, and James says that Abraham was justified by works? That is a question, but doubts are more ambiguous.

So if a parent asks, "What if my children are not elect?" they should not give that kind of thing the time of day. What if they are elect? So questions pursued with an open Bible strengthen our faith; doubts just cause us to chase our tails.

Remember the doctrine of means and ends. God does not ordain things willy-nilly. He has a purpose that attends everything He does. Everything goes back to God, but He ordains the use of instruments or secondary causes to accomplish His purposes. Why does a non-Christian become a Christian? Ultimately, it is because God chose him before the foundation of the world—Jesus died for him two thousand years ago, and the Holy Spirit came into him. We can answer with God's sovereignty in mind, but we can also answer by looking at the means that God used, whether a Bible loaned to him by a roommate, or a tract left in the laundromat, or an evangelistic campaign broadcast on television. We know that these secondary means are not the ultimate cause, but that God in His sovereignty uses such means. In the same way, God is the reason our children will be faithful Christians, but in His sovereignty God uses faithful fathers, and loving mothers, and Christian educations. They are not the final or ultimate cause, but they are one of His *instrumental* causes.

BEGINNING AND ENDING IN FAITH

Trusting God to keep His word does not contradict God's sovereignty. How could it, since God's word is an expression of His sovereignty? Only a sovereign God can make such promises. We must come to Him, trusting that He will keep his word, and accepting the promises regarding our children. We should ask Him to show us any errors in the way we are trusting Him and ask Him to strengthen us where we are weak. We should ask Him to strengthen us accordingly, because children flourish in a confident setting where everything is settled.

If the family is settled in serving God through Jesus Christ, and "that is just what we do, yes ma'am, no questions asked," then we are doing what the Bible says to be doing. By grace through faith, we should seek to create the kind of environment in which these things are simply accepted and believed.

CHAPTER 8

Worldview Parenting

As this is the final chapter of this small book on the covenant home, I wanted to end by discussing worldview parenting. Worldview parenting takes the entire world into account and sees it as the Bible tells us to see it. The world is something that Scripture speaks a lot about—it is what God loved and sent His Son to save. But the word *world* also encompasses the "world system." This is the kind of thing John warns us against: "Love not the world, neither the things that are in the world. If any man love the world, the love of the Father is not in him. For all that is in the world, the lust of the flesh, and the lust of the eyes, and the pride of life, is not of the

Father, but is of the world" (1 John 2:15–16). And this verse should remind us of the temptation in Genesis 3, where Eve is tempted to take the fruit because it is good for food (lust of the flesh), pleasing to the eye (lust of the eyes), and desirous to make wise (pride of life). Worldliness has been with us since the dawn of time, and so of course we still struggle with it today.

When our children are born into this world, our task is to teach them about it and equip them to interact with it, and to stand on their own two feet when they leave home. So how are parents to do that? The world is chasing us all the time through pop-up ads on the internet and through commercials on television and billboards. Christian parents have always had to deal with the temptation to worldliness for their children. That is nothing new, but what is new is how aggressively the world is able to come in and crowd around us with its wares. We might summarize this as the problem of the smartphone and the dumb teenager. The world has always wanted to set traps for teens from believing homes, but now the entire world is contained on a device in that teen's pocket.

The task before us is always to think and live like Christians in everything we touch. If our worldview does not come out in our lives *as actually lived*, it is not Christian worldview thinking at all. Young people today are profoundly shaped by the music they listen to, the movies they watch, and the media they consume. We must therefore equip our children to live as Christians whenever they are out of the house—whether they are going to school for the day or whether they are going off to join the navy—and that includes what kinds of things they consume.

Virtually all Christian parents have to make decisions about social media, movies, YouTube clips, music, and so on. The fundamental question, though, should always be "By what standard?" If a father tells his kid that he does not want him to watch or do something, the instantaneous response from your kid will be "but why?" It will not fly to simply be "uncomfortable" with the music or the movie. Parents have to have these things thought through, and it has to be part of *their* Christian discipleship.

THE PRINCIPLES

Paul says something that is very relevant to this topic: "Finally, brethren, whatsoever things are true, whatsoever things are honest, whatsoever things are just, whatsoever things are pure, whatsoever things are lovely, whatsoever things are of good report; if there be any virtue, and if there be any praise, think on these things" (Phil. 4:8). Paul also says that our thoughts should be on things that are above, not on things that are below (Col. 3:2). Our thoughts should not gravitate to the sewer, or to things that are lowly and base.

Now, there is a difference between things that are *worldly* and things that are *earthly*. God made us material creatures. God could have made food as just a way of refueling, and it could have all been cold porridgy mush with no taste. But God has put us into a world with physical, material pleasures. That is not worldliness, and it is not worldly to be thankful for such material goods; worldliness has to do with the world's system of polishing these things up in such a way that you want to disobey God's law and to pursue His good gifts in all the wrong ways.

The book of Acts describes how many people got rid of their magic books when they were converted: "Many of them also which used curious arts brought their books together, and burned them before all men: and they counted the price of them, and found it fifty thousand pieces of silver" (Acts 19:19). There were a bunch of things in their closets that were not in keeping with a profession of faith in Christ. Many people make fun of fundamentalists for burning their books, and although I do not want to burn any books myself, a lot of Christians would do well to burn some of their books, or at least drive them to the landfill.

Consider the book of Hebrews as well: "But strong meat belongeth to them that are of full age, even those who by reason of use have their senses exercised to discern both good and evil" (Heb. 5:14). There is the distinction between good and evil that everyone can see, but there is also a distinction between good and evil that only a mature Christian can see, and this is because he has been training himself constantly to distinguish good from evil. Many of the issues we are going to raise here are in this category.

PARENTAL AUTHORITY

Before we get into the particulars, I have a few preliminaries that we need to establish. First, God has given parents true authority in the home from the start. Parents are needed, and they are not superfluous. When the kids were little, God provided them with parents so that parents could keep them from running out into the street, or sticking paperclips into electric sockets. It is a basic parental duty to protect them from physical harm and train them in basic obedience. But when the kids get older, and can get pregnant, or buy drugs, or go to jail, many parents do not exercise their authority properly.

When the kids were little and their sins were relatively cute, the world does not end when they disobey. When they flip out in the grocery aisle, they can just be taken home, and when they fall asleep, they look cute again. Many parents therefore indulge sin when it is little and relatively harmless, but after years of indulging the children, the teen years eventually arrive, and now things are really dangerous. Many parents panic at that point and start clamping down rules.

This is entirely backwards: when kids were little, *that* is when they should have learned the basics of moral government. Their teen years are when the restrictions should be taken *off*, because they have been learning how to be self-controlled. Parents *should* take these controls off, but of course this should not be done blindly. Teenagers still need input and direction.

When parents make decisions for the household, they should do it without apology. They must make the decisions wisely, working through the Word of God and applying it, but once they have done so, they should not apologize for it. If they have been indulgent when the kids were little, and then later the regulations start to multiply, that is completely backwards. Again, the job is not to get the kids to conform to the standard. The job is to make them *love* the standard.

OUT OF STEP

We are at war with both modernity and postmodernity. This does not mean a rejection of every feature of modern life, such as running water, electronics, central heating, or medicine. However, it *does* mean taking a stand against all the idolatries that are associated with modernity and postmodernity. This is costly, and as it puts us out of step with a lot of other people, we therefore need the grace of God to strengthen us as we go against the stream.

We particularly need to resist the world's propaganda that says that parents are terminally unhip, and thus unqualified to pass judgment on any of these things. Everyone thinks that young people are street savvy, and that parents know nothing. This is because of unrelenting propaganda that teaches that the kids are of course right, and the parents are eternally clueless. However, parents actually know far more about the world than their kids do, and the concept of "the cool" is a sleight of hand designed to make parents ashamed of themselves. Our responsibility as parents must involve knowing everything that is going on.

Parents should not just ask if the piece of media in question has any bad words in it—the issues are greater than just the moral issues on the surface, although those are included. Parents must not be afraid to include aesthetic and cultural judgments about their child's entertainment as well. When the kids ask to go to *Stupid Movie 3* because "all the kids are going," and you say *no*, the kids will be eager to ask why. Many parents just rush online in order to find a site that counts the *hells, damns,* and tacky scenes. And when they do that, the kids just roll their eyes. Sheesh. They *know* that is not a Christian worldview. C.S. Lewis's *That Hideous Strength* is one of the great novels of the twentieth century, and it has quite a few *hells* and *damns*. To just count profanities is not Christian worldview thinking: it is just skimming along the surface.

What parents should do is tell the kids to go ahead and go, but then tell them they need to be prepared to offer a movie review at dinner the following night. That kid will not have the ability to offer anything like a thoughtful review that engages with the movie, and now they are off to the internet to look up the number of *hells* and *damns* in it. But superficial analysis remains superficial whether the parent is doing it or the kid is. Next time they ask to go to a stupid movie (*Stupid Movie 4*), the parent can just tell them that they are not engaging with the world like a Christian and that they need to learn how to do that first. They need to interact intelligently with what they are being fed. This is not just about profanity counts and bad scenes: it also has to do with plots, aesthetic values, culture, and morality. The reason they can't go to *Stupid Movie 4* is not because their parent has any criticism of the movie (he hasn't seen it). The reason they can't go is because their parent has doubts about the child's critical abilities.

ENGAGING WITH WISDOM

As parents deal with music, movies, social media, and so on, there are several things they should be careful to note. First, avoid dumb distractions. The Christian world for a long time has had no shortage of bogus information on things like rock and roll. For some, the backbeat was the problem, and a generation ago, Christians were worried about messages that were being recorded backwards into the music: the lyrics were saying things like, "I love the devil" or "Go shoot your mom." Leave it to Christians to be more concerned about backwards gibberish than about frontwards wickedness. Avoid dumb distractions; they are not worth it.

Second, avoid legalism. If you say *no* to something and your only reason is "because I said so," then you are teaching legalism. The Bible says that we are to love God with all our *brains*: "And thou shalt love the Lord thy God with all thine heart, and with all thy soul, and with all thy might. And these words, which I command thee this day, shall be in thine heart: and thou shalt teach them diligently unto thy children, and shalt talk of them when thou sittest in thine house, and when thou walkest by the way, and when thou liest down, and when thou risest up. And thou shalt bind them for a sign upon thine hand, and they shall be as frontlets between thine eyes. And thou shalt write them upon the posts of thy house, and on thy gates" (Deut. 6:5–9).

The greatest commandment is therefore given in the context of telling parents to teach their children to love God with all their brains. This includes their literary brains, their mathematical brains, and their historical brains. It also includes their online brains. Everything that they have and are is to be enlisted in the love of God, and this is the way they can learn to love those things that are true and noble. But if their parents set arbitrary standards, they are making up rules detached from the Word of God.

At the same time, just because parents make a decision that their children do not understand yet, that does not mean they are teaching legalism. Parents are often in a position to discern a problem when their children cannot see it. This is because parents are mature, and the kids are immature. Many Christian kids appeal to Christian liberty, and then go and get as close to the line as they possibly can. Then the legalists come along and say, "See: this is why we need rules," and we career right back into rule-making. What we need to do is understand that Christian liberty does *not* mean you get to do whatever you feel. Christian liberty means that you live under the Word of God, and that your parents have the responsibility to teach you to live as a Christian. Christ set us free so that we might do as we ought.

Third, avoid ignorance. Parents should not make their decisions blindly. If they simply go over the lyrics of a song, often the debate would be over at that point. If Mom just printed out the lyrics and offered to read them to Grandma visiting from Iowa, then the child would protest strenuously against the idea. That might be all it takes. I mean, if Spotify knows that a song is raunchy, putting that *Explicit* warning on there, then maybe we can get to a consensus on the subject. Just look at those lyrics—they are obviously vile and obnoxious. Dissensions often occur because parents express vague doubts based on insufficient knowledge, which causes them to ask foggy questions instead of checking things out for themselves. Parents need to know what their kids are listening to and watching, and they need to be engaged with it. And "engaged with it" means knowing what it actually is.

I used to do this with my kids when music videos were first coming out. My kids were in junior high, and so I would turn on a music video. We did not watch the vile, hideous ones, but we would watch one, then I would turn it off, and then say, "What was that? What was the worldview there? What was that saying? Is it true? Did they communicate their message just with lyrics or was it musical?" Parents need to be engaged, and if it is not wholesome enough to engage with, nobody should watch it.

Fourth, avoid sanitized imitations. The evangelical subculture has no shortage of cheap imitations of whatever the world is currently doing. Everything the pagans do, evangelicals can do five years later, and worse. We take the Calvin Klein logo and make a Christ the King logo. We have an eagle eye for whatever the world is doing, except for the heart of what they are doing. I have compared it before to a drunk Japanese businessman singing a song by the Stones on karaoke night. He knows everything about it, the inflections, and the lyrics, except for what it *means*. Evangelicals have a copycat eye for everything except what it means.

On the other hand, we should also avoid reflex contempt for Christian artists, writers, and producers. Many are world-class and at the top of their game, but too many Christians dismiss them with contempt because it is just part of the contemporary Christian scene. Many Christians would rather have worldly lyrics from a vile band than wholesome lyrics from a Christian band that is every bit as good. So the real problem is not technical proficiency, but rather being in love with the world. We should not *care* that the world thinks we do not know what cool is.

Finally, teach the children God has given you. If music is a part of your life (and it should be), you should all sing it together. It should be woven into the fabric of a family's life together, and the parents ought to know enough about the good stuff that schlock is not appealing at all. Talk about the world in the light of Scripture, and do it regularly. Do it when you are driving in the car and when you sit down to dinner. If the kids cannot tell what is wrong with this song or that movie, then they are unprotected. Parents should hold their kids accountable and insist on clarity of thought, rather than excuses, rationalizations, or misty relativism.

CHRISTIAN AESTHETIC RELATIVISM

We need to plead with God that He would give us a knowledge of and love for the beautiful. We all know about the triad of the true, the good, and the beautiful. Reformed believers are not relativistic when it comes to what is true and good, generally speaking. We know that because Jesus is Lord, two plus two always equals four, and that morality does not change from generation to generation. But when it comes to aesthetics, we have capitulated in many ways. If we were to go into many Christian schools, or homeschooling groups, and point out that a particular song is a terrible piece of music, we will frequently get a relativistic response: "Who's to say? Beauty is in the eye of the beholder." That kind of thing is straight from the Pit, and that is why it smells like sulfur. If we are answering in that way, it is because we have given in to relativism when it comes to aesthetic judgment, and it is only a matter of time before the next defenses will fall.

Now, suppose I said that someone's favorite band sounds like a helicopter landing sideways on a tin bridge, but they answer me by pointing to the complex rhythms, and the allusions to the Psalms in the lyrics, and how the bassist graduated from Juilliard. The central issue is not whether he is right or I am wrong. We should rejoice first in the fact that this is a debate that Christians can have. This is because he is pointing to things that I might be overlooking, and he is acknowledging that there are such things as objective aesthetic standards. But if he says, "That's just your opinion, man," then it is game over. That person is not in a position to resist any relativistic goo in any area . . . because he has granted the authority of the subjective response. But we are Christians, and we must honor the Word of God in every area of life. Musical relativism should be as appalling to us as any other kind of relativism.

This does not mean that there are not such things as different tastes. Not everyone enjoys *all* the food at the international food fair, and the world is a complex place. Aesthetics is a subtle discipline, but there still remains a fixed value. God knows what is lovely and wholesome, and He wants us to grow in that knowledge and to bring up our children into it with us.

CONCLUSION

Near the beginning, I said that a covenant was a solemn bond, sovereignly administered, with attendant blessings and curses. As we have worked through the material in this short book, it is important to remember that whenever we were addressing sins, or duties, or responsibilities, we were talking about the *standards* imposed by that "solemn bond." But we must also remember that God is the covenant-keeping God, and He has not just thrown us into the covenant in order to fend for ourselves. He has made numerous covenant promises, found throughout Scripture, and we know that He always keeps His promises. This is what makes covenant-keeping by parents a matter of grace. God assigns our duties to us in the covenant, and He fulfills our duties for us as we walk by faith. Work out your salvation, Paul says, with fear and trembling, for God is at work in you to will and to do for His good pleasure (Phil 2:12–13). As we look at our (very challenging) parental duties, we must keep covenant, doing so by faith. This means we work out the good works that God has prepared beforehand for us to do, and we do this knowing that He is at work in us to will and to do. We do parental good works because we are God's workmanship (Eph. 2:10). And we should rest in that.

Made in the USA
Middletown, DE
23 November 2022

15460813R00087